திருக்குறள்
TIRUKKUṞAḶ

இன்பத்துப்பால்
INPATTU-P-PĀL

காமத்துப்பால்
KĀMATTU-P-PĀL

திருவள்ளுவர்
Tiruvaḷḷuvar

THE BOOK *of* DESIRE

Tiruvalluvar

Translated from the Tamil by
MEENA KANDASAMY

GALLEY BEGGAR PRESS

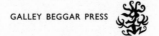

First published in 2023
by Galley Beggar Press Limited
37 Dover Street, Norwich NR2 3LG

A CIP for this book is available from the British Library

Paperback ISBN: 978-1-913111-36-6
Black-cover edition ISBN: 978-1-913111-40-3

Text and design by Tetragon, London
Printed and bound in Great Britain by CPI Books, Chatham

Dedicated to Appa, Dr Kandasamy

One summer vacation in my teenage years
you made me read, and learn by rote,
every single kuṟaḷ.
I never realised it then,
but that changed everything . . .

CONTENTS

INTRODUCTION

Would I Quarrel, Would I Embrace?

TRANSLATING THE LOVE POETRY OF *TIRUKKUṞAḶ* AS A TAMIL DECOLONIAL FEMINIST[1]

One of the world's oldest surviving languages, Tamil, is spoken by about 78 million people in the south Indian states of Tamil Nadu and Puducherry, Eelam, and elsewhere globally. Modern linguistic scholarship places the oldest extant Tamil literature at around 300 BCE. Reflective of the Tamil philosophy of life, the *Tirukkuṟaḷ* (composed in the first century BCE) is the most vital text of this ancient civilisation – a heartbeat to its culture and imagination. Authored by Tiruvaḷḷuvar, no biographical details of the poet remain. Anonymity does not mean obscurity; this is a poet who remains central to our everyday lives. Recognising him as the greatest historical Tamil icon, the state of Tamil Nadu officially follows a Tamil calendar that begins in the year 31 BCE, believed to be the year of Tiruvaḷḷuvar's birth. In his memory, we keep time; through his poetry, we navigate our world.

The 1330 verses of the *Tirukkuṟaḷ* are divided into three sections: Morality, Materialism and Desire. Written in the kuṟaḷ venpa, each kuṟaḷ runs into two lines: the first consists of four feet, and the second of three. The third section, the Iṉpattuppāl

(Book of Desire) translated here, consists of 250 kuṟaḷs divided into 25 chapters. The first translation of the *Tirukkuṟaḷ* in English appeared more than 220 years ago, in 1794. It remains one of the most widely translated non-religious texts. In the intervening years, more than 100 translations have appeared in English.

Here, I have attempted the first feminist interventionist translation into English – remaining true to the female (and male) desire throbbing through the lifeblood of this text, while retaining the drama that pervades the quintessential Tamil world of exaggerated hurt, lovers' quarrels and evenings lost to longing. Reading the Iṉpattuppāl, the erotic poetry of the *Tirukkuṟaḷ*, is an enriching, unforgettable experience. I invite you to partake of its beauty.

The kuṟaḷ that opens the Book of Desire describes the first encounter with its heroine. Dazzled, the hero wonders if this woman is a fearsome goddess. When she faces off with him in the second kuṟaḷ, he feels that she has brought along a 'shock troop of terrifying goddesses'. By the third kuṟaḷ, he confesses that he, who has never known death, now realises that death wages war with a woman's beautiful eyes. In a later kuṟaḷ, her eyes devour lives. Fatally attractive, she strikes fear and terror in her beholder, arresting their attention.

This deadly, intoxicating woman in the *Tirukkuṟaḷ* is a Tamil woman. She might be a universal stand-in for the beloved, but she was conceived in the Tamil universe.

When the *hero* encounters this Tamil woman, he is awe-struck, almost afraid of the powers she holds. How does the *reader* encounter this Tamil woman? Not face-to-face, as in a physical or imagined encounter, but in the realm of ideas, where her beauty is dismissed as a distraction.

Does this fear-inducing Tamil beauty have the right to comment about the text in which she appears and holds court?

Does this woman ever exist outside of the text?

I ask these questions because that terrifying (Tamil) goddess is absent. Absent as a translator. Absent as a commentator. Absent as a philosopher of love. Absent as an aesthetic spokesperson.

Isn't this absence of women – as translators, as commentators – a product of marginalisation and masculine insecurity, a gatekeeping of the world of literature? Or is the goddess' silence a confirmation of the fact that women writers have been reduced to their subjective positions, forced by patriarchy into shunning the universal while flaunting a preference for the granular world of the particular? Will she, in her paratextual incarnation, strike terror? In this intellectual encounter, is she seductive, striking, or both?

Does this, eventually, lead to love?

Here, in the pages of this book, I claim for myself the space to interpret the Tamil woman in the *Tirukkuṟaḷ*. As a woman in love, I also claim the space to be her. This is a recursive loop.

When it comes to the language of love, my Tamil lovers only need a reference, a citation, screenshots of whichever kuṟaḷ suits the mood of the moment. My other lovers, at least the ones who are capable of taking the heat from terrifying goddesses, the ones who have been strong enough to handle me, require a translation of intimacy, culture, gloss.

As I write, I realise that I have been translating this Tamil universe since long before I conceived of it as a literary, political project.

I confess, I am a writer who glosses out of habit. Sometimes, providing the gloss to my culture and literature serves as seduction. Most often, this gloss is how I demarcate boundaries. This gloss, this demarcation, this difference, is how I come into my own. This is how I tell the world, in whatever small and feeble way, that we are a culture, we are a civilisation, that we have existed for a long time and we are here to stay. Writing in English means a broader audience, but it does not have to mean the end of my Tamilness. On the contrary, I often feel that I have something to say precisely because I am Tamil. My Tamilness is where my life as a writer-translator begins.

What do I think as I sit down to write this introduction? I started translating the love poetry of the *Tirukkuṟaḷ* on 23 April 2012, a full decade ago. There was nothing rushed about this project – I came to it again and again, layering up the meaning where it felt necessary, paring it down to the bare bones to reflect the exact Tamil, where brutal brevity worked best. There is nothing that I am going to be setting forth here that I have not done in the translation itself, so in writing this preface I feel awkward and torn. The Book of Desire is pure love poetry. My every impulse says to leave the lovers alone, to let them live in their little world. The poetry is enough, it has withstood the test of time, and, with any luck, its beauty will continue to be exchanged between lovers across languages, across cultures and continents.

Why then do I write this introduction, this political framing of the text, even as I'm disturbed by the incongruence of the attempt? Do not ruin the romance, I remind myself. I have read these verses over and over again, and there is a part of me which feels that no one needs to know anything about Tamil at all, about its antiquity or beauty, about its history of resistance or renaissance, to appreciate their human drama. There is also the Tamil woman in me, who thinks: this is the universe

I know, the one into which I was born, in which I have been loved, learned to love and been through heartbreak; what if my universal is singular, exceptional, and different from others? This is a facet of life that I have encountered often – never wanting to be exoticised, but aware that in other lands I'm a stranger, nonetheless.

So.

Tamil is the world's oldest classical language still in use. It belongs to the Dravidian family of languages, which is estimated to be at least 4500 years old.[2] Linguistically distinct and independent from the Indo-European languages spoken in the Indian subcontinent, Tamil's origin story has endowed its people with a unique history, culture and political character. As Tamils, we also lay claim to being the oldest unbroken, surviving civilisation. A study published in *Nature*[3] shows how primitive stone tools found at Athirampakkam, 60 kilometres from the state capital of Chennai, have been dated to around 385,000 years old. These Stone Age artefacts are 'older than the oldest known *Homo sapiens* fossils found in [...] outside Africa'. Similarly, iron artefacts found at Mayiladumparai in Tamil Nadu have been radiocarbon-dated to 2172 BCE (4200 years ago), making it the oldest Iron Age site in India.

Ongoing explorations at Keezhadi in southern Tamil Nadu date the existence of a civilisation there to 3200 years ago. Scripts and evidence of extensive literacy unearthed in this Keezhadi excavation have led to theories that the Sangam (Caṅkam; i.e., classical) era, believed to have started around 300 BCE, could stretch back as far as 600 BCE. Many of these findings have come to light in recent years, although sites such as Adichanallur in Thoothukkudi were discovered as early as 1876. The seaport of Korkai mentioned in Sangam literature, for instance, correlates with Korkai near Adichanallur. The regrettable fact that these discoveries are being made so late in the day is partly owing to apathy, but also to the fact that many of the artefacts unearthed in the colonial period were taken to museums in Europe.

Colonialism was the first rupture in the continuous, unbroken tradition of the Tamil language's status and usage within Tamil civilisation. In addition to their territorial contiguity, the Tamil states preserved their linguistic originality. Te Po Meenkshisunadaranar, a renowned scholar of the Tamil language (who also wrote on the philosophy of the *Tirukkuṟaḷ*), wrote that, throughout their history, 'Tamil people as a rule had Tamil as the language of the state, science, art or literature', as opposed to other parts of India where the official language was either Persian, one of the Prakrits or Sanskrit, which was unknown to the majority of the people.[4] Today, when the Tamil language and its people are seen as a bulwark in resisting the communal and religious divides that have engulfed the entire Indian subcontinent, these histories gain tremendous importance. Of the problems of the national language in Tamil Nadu, the linguist and scholar of Tamil M.S. Andronov writes, 'The age-old tradition of using the native tongue in all spheres of social and cultural life was violated only in the last 100–150 years during the country's dependence on Britain.'[5] He cites Tamil writer Mu Varadarajan in this respect, 'From time immemorial till Clive [presumably Robert Clive, one of the most controversial colonial figures] Tamilnad remained a country whose state language was Tamil. It is difficult to find in world history other examples of one and the same language functioning as a state language for such a long period of time'. Foreign policy commentators have described how Tamils are 'inordinately proud and defensively anxious about the merits of their literary heritage', emphasising the necessity that the Tamil language 'be supported as a shield against the claims of Hindi and as a monument of regional nationalism'.[6] I plead guilty to these charges (although I do not think we are any more proud or anxious than, say, the French). Having covered the bare bones of Tamil's antiquity, let me rest my case and move on.

Now. We move from language to literature.

Eventually, to the book in question.

The Tamil scholar Kamil Zvelebil notes that Tamil began to be cultivated as a literary language around the fourth or third century BCE, following the disintegration of the Proto-South-Dravidian linguistic unity between the eighth and sixth centuries BCE.[7] Commenting on Tamil literature, he observes:

> The earliest literature in Tamil is a model unto itself – it is absolutely unique in the sense that, in subject-matter, thought-content, language and form, it is entirely and fully indigenous, that is, Tamil. [...] And not only that: it is only the Tamil culture that has produced – uniquely so in India – an independent literary theory of a very high standard, including metrics and prosody, poetics and rhetoric.

Revisiting his claim about what sets apart classical Tamil literature, Zvelebil writes:

> First of all, Tamil is probably the one ancient language of India that bears the reflection of the life of an entire people; that is, its heroes are idealised types derived from what we might even call 'common folk'. Classical (i.e. the so-called *Caṅkam*) Tamil literature is not the literature of the barons; neither is it the literature of a monastic order; nor the literature of an

élite, of a *nāgarika*; it is thus not the literature of a particular social class.

Even as Tamil writing contains 'the whole gamut of basic human experience', Zvelebil is keen to clarify that classical Tamil literature is not a *Volksliteratur* (folk literature), but rather a *Kunstdichtung* (art writing).[8]

Tirukkuṟaḷ as a text belongs to this lineage of Caṅkam poetry. Authored by Tiruvaḷḷuvar, a poet about whom few authentic biographical details have survived, the text too maintains opacity, giving away nothing about its author. The *Tirukkuṟaḷ* has occupied an honoured place in the Tamil literary canon, with quotations used verbatim or alluded to in classic epics such as the *Cilappatikāram* (fifth century CE), the *Maṇimēkalai* (sixth century CE) and the *Kamba Ramayanam* (ninth to 12th century CE) onwards. More commentaries have been written on the *Tirukkuṟaḷ* than on any other Tamil text.[9] The ten most important medieval commentators (all male) are remembered through a standalone anonymous verse,[10] and only five of their commentaries are available in full today. The vagaries of time mean that much has been lost forever. However, every generation has infused fresh blood into the *Tirukkuṟaḷ*: writing a commentary or attempting a translation is a favoured pastime of retired diplomats and reigning chief ministers. Some modern commentaries, such as Tamil scholar Mu Varadarajan's accessible version, have become runaway bestsellers in Tamil Nadu, going into hundreds of reprints in less than a century.[11]

The 1330 verses of the *Tirukkuṟaḷ* are divided into three sections (Aram, Porul and Iṉpam, denoting Morality, Materialism and Desire respectively). If the first two parts of the *Tirukkuṟaḷ* can be described as a discourse on 'how one ought to live', the third sidesteps that didacticism. Instead of pontificating on 'how one ought to love', the text presents a pair of lovers: anonymous, universal, absolutely democratic.

The lines of poetry in the *Tirukkuṟaḷ* are composed in the kuṟaḷ venpa, an ancient metrical form dating to the Sangam era and one of the most difficult stanzaic structures of Tamil prosody. The third section, the Iṉpattuppāl or Kāmattuppāl, literally means the *Section on Love*. (Although *Iṉpam* suggests happiness or pleasure in the original Tamil, I decided to forego the word 'pleasure' in this translation; somehow the English carries an altogether different connotation, and I did not want to mislead anyone into thinking that this is a technical manual on how to reach an orgasm!)

The Iṉpattuppāl consists of 250 kuṟaḷs divided into 25 chapters. It is important to remind the reader here that the order of the chapters, as well as the order of the individual kuṟaḷs within them, differs depending on the commentator. François Gros boldly reordered the Iṉpattuppāl for his French translation, choosing to shuffle the twenty-five chapters into five sections based on the akam[12] conventions of landscape and mood (five regions, five states of love). With this singular exception, the third section of the *Tirukkuṟaḷ* has always followed the same sequence in translation. For the purposes of this book, I am following the standard chapterisation in which all books of the *Tirukkuṟaḷ* presently in print exist, based on the commentary and arrangement by Parimēlaḻakar. Because Parimēlaḻakar has been taken as the authority, and despite the remarkable range of variance from one commentator to another, a standardisation has set in.[13] (Parimēlaḻakar means 'the handsome man on a horse'; remember his name, more on him to come.)

What is a kuṟaḷ? A poem in two lines. The first line consists of four feet (cīr, in Tamil), and the second of three. A *cīr* is a metrical foot, consisting of up to four acai (metreme), and forming part of the ati (or metrical line) itself. On my website, https://www.kandasamy.co.uk/the-book-of-desire, I have explained the exigencies of Tamil metrics, interior rhyme, and the matrix in which each kuṟaḷ is cast. This formal rigour and its intimate connection to the subject matter ensures that the kuṟaḷs lend themselves to easy memorisation, making them some of the most quoted poetry and epigrams on Tamil public platforms. While the complex construction of a kuṟaḷ according to the rules of its venpa, one of many forms of Tamil classical poetry, might appear exacting, strenuous and clinical, anyone can partake of its beauty without realising the depth of its foundational grammatical rules; kuṟaḷs appear effortlessly graceful. I resist easy, offhand comparisons to the haiku, the doha or the couplet because the kuṟaḷ is unique to Tamil, and I feel that the form should be referred to as it is in the language and culture from which it arises.

To capture the beauty of the kuṟaḷs, the scholar of Tamil François Gros channels Tamil littérateurs:

> Brief and dense, each *kuṟaḷ*, or short couplet, is a multi-faceted diamond; in Tamil terms, it is the dewdrop on the blade of millet which reflects the towering palm tree, the hollowed out mustard seed which encloses the seven seas, or the atom which contains the whole universe.[14]

Even as I wax eloquent about the Tamil language and the *Tirukkuṟaḷ* here, some more ground needs to be covered: how did the *Tirukkuṟaḷ* survive all these years? If this text is a living text today, we owe an ongoing debt for its intergenerational transmission over thousands of years, to every scribe who copied it onto palm-leaf manuscripts, every publisher who keeps the *Tirukkuṟaḷ* in print, every translator, every commentator, every enterprising spirit who renders it as a pocket-sized book or as an app, every elder who gifts the book to newly married couples at weddings; to over-enthusiastic Tamil teachers who make students learn it every day and recite it in the morning assembly, to the High Court judge who ruled that it be mandatory on the school syllabus.[15] As a text so much in contemporary usage, quoted so often, taught across the state, painted inside every government bus, with Tamil television channels airing five-minute commentary on a kuṟaḷ every morning, one could easily forget how the *Tirukkuṟaḷ* was handed down through the ages. History is easier to trace if we begin with the advent of the printing press: the book was first printed in 1812 by Thanjai Gnanaprakasam. In 1850, Vedagiri Mudaliar printed the first complete edition of the *Tirukkuṟaḷ* with commentaries, followed by a revised edition in 1853. In pre-modern times, the *Tirukkuṟaḷ* survived in the form of palm-leaf manuscripts.[16] Being organic material, highly susceptible to humidity and termites, as well as regular wear and tear, they had a lifespan of a couple of hundred years at best. As such, manuscripts were meticulously copied and thus preserved for posterity (or at least that was the plan, until the socio-political climate started to go awry).

Entwined in this story is the story of the Tamil script. Each transcription of a kuṟaḷ meant rendering it in whichever script was in use at the time. It is said that the deeply cursive and rounded nature of the Tamil writing system was an adaptation to the usage of palm leaves as the writing medium; harsh, straight and angular letters inscribed with a stylus ran the risk of tearing the manuscripts. The Tamil of Tiruvaḷḷuvar's time is intelligible even today – some archaic words have fallen into disuse, but not beyond the realm of resuscitation. Because Tamil as a language is agglutinative, it builds upon its root words; while some might have morphed into other meanings, they have not disappeared. If you're curious to know how renderings of the *Tirukkuṟaḷ* have looked through the ages, I recommend *Tirukkuṟaḷ in Ancient Scripts* (1980) by Siromoney, Govindaraju and Chandrasekaran.[17] I also recommend 'Jinavani', an Android app that allows you to render any line of Tamil in the Tamil-Brahmi and the Vatteluttu scripts. But while this is endlessly fascinating, I do not want to lose or leave my reader here. I want you to come back with me to the story of the palm-leaf manuscripts.

'When you lift a palm-leaf manuscript, the edge breaks. When you untie a knot, the leaf cracks. When you turn a leaf, it breaks in half... All old manuscripts are falling apart, one after the other, and there is no one to make new copies.' So wrote the Tamil scholar S.V. Damodaram Pillai in 1887, as he lamented the loss of manuscripts to fire, water, religious taboo, termites, insects and the earth.[18] Recently, a video clip tracing the story of how the *Tirukkuṟaḷ* was rescued from permanent oblivion went viral online. In it, the senior Tamil scholar Senthalai Na Gowthaman explains how Tamil people were told that throwing their palm-leaf manuscripts into the river on the festival day of Aadi Perukku (the 18th day in the Tamil month of Aadi, mid-July) would give them moksham (a break from the cycle of birth and rebirth, a shorthand for heaven). Gowthaman goes on to describe how destroying the manuscripts was 'cynically encouraged' as a sport among 'gullible people', wherein multiple palm-leaf manuscripts containing Sanskrit and Tamil texts were dropped into the river at once, as if in a competition to see which texts would go the farthest. Wrapped in water-repellent root-fibre, the Sanskrit manuscripts would float right back; meanwhile the Tamil masses, ignorant of these designs, lost all their knowledge. Consigned to the water (or burnt as firewood), the regular reproduction of these manuscripts stopped and many were lost forever. This is a story I have heard repeated again and again on public platforms. As a philosophy, Brahminism sanctified the denial of knowledge; as a practice, it ensured that existing knowledge among other egalitarian cultures was also taken away. Today, the destruction of indigenous Tamil knowledge by Brahminical forces forms a collective memory of humiliation.

Aware that no argument holds water unless it also carries rigorous citation, I got my hands on a 300-page book published in 1959 – *Maṟaintu Pōṉa Tamiḻ Nūlkaḷ* (translating as *Tamil Texts That Have Disappeared*) by the scholar Mayilai Cīṉi Vēṅkaṭacāmi. Vēṅkaṭacāmi begins his preface with a tragic episode: lacking biological children, he adopts Anbazhagan (a three-year-old boy) and Thankamani (a one-and-a-half-year-old girl). When the children die tragically young, he is left grief-stricken. Seeking consolation, he tries to immerse himself in reading the *Yāpparuṅkala Virutti*, a commentary on an 11th century grammatical treatise. In the course of reading, Vēṅkaṭacāmi realises that the commentator frequently cites old books, many of which have been lost to history. With the death of his two children fresh in his mind, he imagines every forgotten book as a child irretrievably lost by Mother Tamil and begins to collect details of the texts. Vēṅkaṭacāmi's story reminds me of the fictional experiments of Bolaño and Borges, except that his was painfully real. In *Maraintu Pōṉa Tamiḻ Nūlkaḷ*, Vēṅkaṭacāmi collates his list of cross-cited Tamil texts that had been lost, including their titles and whatever information and excerpts were still available from them. The book notes more than 100 literary texts (including 50 books of love poetry, war poetry and epics, and 67 miscellaneous texts), nine on music, 34 of Tamil drama, and 45 commentaries on Tamil grammar or linguistics. Vēṅkaṭacāmi also provides an appendix of books whose titles weren't known, and those for which no information existed at all. At the end of this well-documented and irrefutable chronicle of loss, around page 360, Vēṅkaṭacāmi begins to lay bare the reasons for this mass disappearance, citing several anecdotes from the life of Tamil revivalist scholar U.V. Swaminatha Aiyar, who went in search of these palm-leaf manuscripts and others. I condense them here to the scale of a Twitter thread: natural calamity; natural causes; militant Brahminical Hinduism[19] and religious hatred; people superstitiously throwing away manuscripts into the rivers and sea at Aadi Perukku; the children of Tamil scholars not realising the value of the knowledge contained in these works and clearing them out; custodians of these manuscripts in temples feeding them into the fire as a part of Brahminical rituals. Where these works escaped such organised destruction, their contents were mercilessly mauled. Charles Gover, a British folklorist and one of the earliest translators of the *Tirukkuṟaḷ*, wrote in 1871:

> It is almost impossible now to obtain a printed copy of any early Tamil book that has not been systematically corrupted and mutilated, to meet the views of those whose livelihood depends on the rejection by the public of Dravidian literature and its acceptance of the Puranic legends.

Gover's subtle formulation, 'those whose livelihood depends on the rejection by the public of Dravidian literature and its acceptance of the Puranic legends,' is perhaps the politest way of calling out Brahmins and Sanatana Dharma I have yet encountered. But even Gover steps out of his English reserve soon enough:

> The Brahmans corrupted what they could not destroy. The editing of all books gradually fell to them, because they alone had the leisure and knowledge that literary labour required [...]. This process was continued till it became almost impossible to discover the original [...]. The only copies that I have been able to purchase are as obscure and overloaded with puranic superstition as the legend of any pagoda. The same thing has occurred with all the best Dravidian poetry.[20]

It is a miracle then, under these exenterating circumstances, that the *Tirukkuṟaḷ* survived at all. It was one such palm-leaf manuscript that finally reached Francis Whyte Ellis (1777–1819), a British civil servant in the Madras Presidency who was also a scholar of Tamil. Deeply invested in the language and literature, Ellis was the first person to classify the Dravidian languages as belonging to a separate language family, a theoretical contribution for which Robert Caldwell (often credited with the breakthrough) acknowledges him. Ellis founded the St George College Press in Madras, and the first book he printed was Beschi's Tamil grammar *Kodum Tamil* in 1813. Before his untimely death from cholera, he published his own translation of the *Tirukkuṟaḷ*. The Tamil inscription on Ellis's grave marks his love of the *Tirukkuṟaḷ*, as did his actions in life: when he was in charge of the Madras treasury and mint, he issued a gold coin bearing Tiruvaḷḷuvar's image, and in 1818, when Madras suffered a drinking-water shortage, Ellis dug 27 wells. One bears a long inscription where Ellis praises the poet, quoting Kuṟaḷ 737 as inspiration for the project.[21]

The first English translation of the *Tirukkuṟaḷ* was a partial one by N.E. Kindersley, appearing more than 220 years ago in 1794. Francis Whyte Ellis attempted a translation of 120 couplets – 69 in verse and 51 in prose – in the year 1812. In the intervening years, more than 100 translations have appeared in English.[22] So far, only one of these translators has been a woman. For those who wish to read a detailed history of the early translations of the *Tirukkuṟaḷ* and their publication in Europe, I suggest George Uglow Pope's *The 'Sacred' Kurral of Tiruvalluva-Nayanar* (1886), fully digitised and available online.[23]

Pope was truly enamoured by the *Tirukkuṟaḷ*. He compared it to the gnomic poetry of Greece, composed a sonnet in honour of Vaḷḷuvar,[24] and went on to declare that in value the *Tirukkuṟaḷ* 'far outweighs the whole of the remaining Tamil literature', calling it 'one of the select number of great works which have entered into the very soul of a whole people, and which can never die'.[25] Pope was simultaneously condescending: 'Many of these epigrammatic masterpieces have a profound significance, of which their author himself was hardly conscious'. While he tried hard to claim a Christian influence for Vaḷḷuvar, he wasn't the first to do so. Despite efforts from many quarters to claim Tiruvaḷḷuvar as one of their own, including by the Shaivite, Vaishnavaite, Buddhist, Jainist and Christian religious traditions, the non-denominational nature of its verses mean that the *Tirukkuṟaḷ* has remained a universal text.

Tiru- is an honorific prefix in Tamil, and Vaḷḷuvar is the specific caste name of the soothsayers/priests of the Paraiyars of Tamil Nadu, a people once considered untouchable. Valentine Daniel writes of how 'they lay special claim to this famous poet', considering him their own ancestor.[26] Delving into the historical anecdotes still available at the time of his writing, Pope notes:

> It is strange that the title by which alone the greatest poet of South India is known should be one indicating an origin most degrading and contemptible in the eyes of the vast multitudes of whom he has been for ten centuries the Oracle. The last has indeed become first.[27]

Why speak of caste in a book that speaks of love? Why speak of caste in a book that rejects the inequality of birth, declaring '*piṟappokkum ellā uyirkkum*' (Kuṟaḷ 972): all lives are equal by birth? Caste has become embedded in the history of our literature and in the story of our lives. Let me bring you another palm-leaf episode, another slice of history demonstrating how Brahminism (in the guise of Hinduism) worked against the Tamil language. The Dikshitars of Chidambaram are a Brahmin caste that hereditarily control the Natarajar temple to this day, refusing to divulge temple accounts even to state authorities.[28] In the 10th century CE, they refused to part with palm-leaf manuscripts of Tamil hymns kept locked away in the temple chambers, even though the demand came from King Rajaraja Cholan. They argued that unless the four legendary (long-dead) Tamil scholars – Appar, Sambandar, Sundarar and Manikavachagar – came together with the King and demanded the palm-leaf manuscripts, the Brahmin custodians of the temple would not give them up. Rajaraja Cholan was unfazed. He made life-size golden icons of the scholars, brought them in a procession to the temple and demanded the release of the manuscripts. (It is interesting to think of the conceit here. What if the Dikshitars had refused, on the grounds that the statues were artificial rather than alive? I like to think that if they had, Rajaraja Cholan would have done the same to the Natarajar statue, the temple's own object of worship.) As it was, the Brahmins were forced to buckle under the pressure of a mighty state, and the manuscripts were retrieved. We might have come a long way since the 10th century, but not the Dikshitars, who maintain that temple in a chokehold of anti-Tamil hatred and Brahminical superiority. Even today, the Dikshitars there do not allow prayers in the Tamil language, something that has been the subject of long-running litigation. Jayasheela, a Dalit woman who attempted to offer prayers in Tamil, was assaulted by these Dikshitar priests just a few months ago.[29] Incidents like this undermine claims that the Sanskrit–Tamil divide is something that belongs to the haunted past.

Circling back to the *Tirukkuṟaḷ*, and keeping with the theme of palm-leaf manuscripts, here is another revelation. The manuscript that reached the hands of Francis Whyte Ellis was printed and subsequently took on a life of its own, but the earliest reference to palm-leaf manuscripts about the *Tirukkuṟaḷ* reaches further back in time. Sent by the Danish King Frederick IV to Tranquebar (modern-day Tharangambadi) as a missionary, German-born Bartholomäus Ziegenbalg was among the first Europeans to study the Tamil language, going on to publish the *Grammatica Damulica* (1716), one of the earliest works on Tamil printed in Europe. Ziegenbalg was a truly incredible character – he writes of starting a school in his house 'which accommodates more girls than boys' and charmingly insists 'I am quite confident the girls will be able to hold their own against the boys'. In order to build his library of local texts, he attempts to get scribes to copy the palm-leaf manuscripts before realising that it is easier to buy them from Brahmin widows living in the neighbourhood. What has survived today is not his library but a catalogue of it, which mentions the *Tirukkuṟaḷ*. I quote his words verbatim, because they capture the book's place in society:

> A book on morals in verse form, by its material not unlike the writings of Seneca. The Malabaris think very highly of it and it is indeed one of the most learned and edifying books found among them. High-class Malabaris often make it their handbook and whenever one enters into a discussion with them they are always ready to quote a few verses from it to prove the validity of their words. It is the habit of educated Malabaris to confirm and demonstrate everything with one or the other verse; to do so is considered a great art amongst them. Therefore such books are not just read but learnt by heart. The poet I have in my house knows this book by heart and many other difficult books too, and though he is blind, he can still recite them quite accurately. The author of this book was called Diruwalliwer, he was a noble poet and lived in the same place where the holy Apostle Thomas had lived and preached the Gospel. In the opinion of the poets this book is one and a half thousand years old. The verses are very short and thoughtful; quite often one single verse covers a considerable amount of material. Only advanced schools teach this book since it would be much too difficult for young people.[30]

Far ahead of his time, Ziegenbalg's literary works and his German–Tamil/Tamil–German dictionary have been lost forever. After all, he arrived in India a century before Indology had established itself as a rigorous academic discipline; still, what better way to discuss Indology than to scandalise the field even further?

In researching this essay, I learnt that Ziegenbalg 'was aware of the Vedas and their significance for Brahmins, but he found Tamil texts more important for most of those he sought to convert, and he seems never to have regarded it as important even to learn Sanskrit'.[31] I was also surprised to discover that the actual Vedas did not reach Europe until the 18th century. What's more, and although they were catalogued by Jesuits in 1739, they remained unread for decades. Will Sweetman writes how the 'desire for the Vedas expressed from Europe' seized these missionaries even 'at the very time that, in their hands, Ziegenbalg's Tamil library was falling into ruin'. The reputation of the Vedas in Europe around the turn of the 18th century demonstrates what Dorothy Figueria has aptly called 'the authority of an absent text'. The books erroneously considered to be Vedas – texts on which the divinity, knowledge, and supposed monotheism of the native Indians had been based since the 1520s – were in fact Tamil, and they included the *Tirukkuṟaḷ*.

In an engaging research paper, Sweetman traces the construction of the Vedas' textual authority, demonstrating how the Brahmins' unwillingness to share them and the Vedas' in-built intransmissibility came to compound their perceived sacredness. For those unfamiliar with India's caste system, knowledge of the Vedas is a privilege only afforded to the Brahmins; codifications of law such as the Manusmriti even prescribe that the low-caste person who hears a Veda must have molten lead poured into his ears. Sweetman's research establishes that, until well into the 18th century, the view from Europe was shaped primarily by just one early report. This was contained in an account of 'the opinions, rites and ceremonies of the Gentiles of India', written by a Portuguese friar, Agostinho de Azevedo, most likely in the late 1580s. His brief statement on the Vedas was recycled in every major European language throughout the 17th century and even into the 18th, 50 years after the first manuscripts of the Vedas had arrived in Europe. In fact, like almost all missionaries writing on Hinduism prior to the 1720s, Azevedo relied on vernacular – in his case, Tamil – texts for his own account of Indian religious belief. References to these sources were, however, excised by those who repeatedly plagiarised his account. Sweetman further writes:

> Despite his claim, then, that the Vedas are the original scriptures that prescribe what the gentiles of India are to believe and what rites they are to perform, Azevedo's actual sources are all much later Tamil sources: Tirumantiram, Tiruvācakam, Tivākaram, *Tirukkuṟaḷ*, and the text on caste. This combination – identification of the Vedas as the oldest authoritative sources, together with a reliance on quite different texts for the actual details of the religious practices of those who so acknowledged the Vedas – would be repeated in the works of many of those who wrote from India. But the identification of the Vedas as the oldest and most authoritative works meant that it was only the Vedas that gained widespread recognition in Europe as the sacred texts of the Indians.[32]

Sweetman's research may be marginal to our appreciation of the love poetry of the *Tirukkuṟaḷ,* but these startling revelations are devastating when we understand them in the broader context of colonialism.

If translation is to be to be a decolonial practice, it also calls for us to widen the scope of what colonialism is, and what it involves. Colonialism to me is not only white-skinned European hegemony. Colonialism is subjugation and supremacy; colonialism is the inflated superiority of claiming to be a better civilisation; colonialism is the imposition of another set of cultural values; colonialism is the restructuring of a society based on the hierarchies prevalent in the coloniser's own. In this context, colonialism to me is the inroads made by the patriarchal caste system into Tamil culture and society. Colonialism is erasure and appropriation; colonialism is the attempt to subsume. Sanskrit and Sanatana Dharma (the hierarchal social order of inequality based on caste and misogyny) have been one of the chief colonisers where Tamil people are concerned. Hindi, supported by right-wing Hindu nationalism, is another. British, Dutch, French colonialism are also actors, but they are not the only ones who eviscerated the lives of my people. Colonialism is thus also a violent project of caste and misogyny being forced down the throat of another civilisation by overt and covert means, one which does not get the same attention as British colonialism or other such offensive campaigns of oppression unleashed by white people. Because I see translation as a radical and transformative act of political intervention, I shoulder the burden of calling out these colonisers also. I do not believe that just because we are all brown folk, just because we have all been colonised by the British, we ought to maintain a culture of silence and soft-pedalling about these violent histories within our own traditions. Framing translation as a dynamic dismantling of colonial traditions, I am not going to remain tight-lipped just because one coloniser shares the colour of my skin and the other does not. Decolonialisation for me is not a blind return to indigeneity – because what indigeneity are we talking about? If we exorcise the ghosts of British colonialism, are we content with a de facto second-class status, with Tamil being referred to as a *neecha baasha* (a low language) by the Brahminical class, forbidden from being used in worship in temples all over Tamil Nadu? If colonialism is erasure, we need to wonder who caused the first disappearance of Tamil texts, and consequently Tamil history. Answering this question will reveal who the earliest colonial power upon my people was.

Brahmin academics in Western universities who lead the bandwagon of decolonial studies will not raise these questions. When someone like me raises them, they will resort to hand-wringing, blame me for pandering to the West, label me a Tamil fanatic, or simply give me the silent treatment. The more sophisticated among them talk about the syncretistic nature and synchronicity of all traditions – this is a deflection mechanism, a historical amnesia. A failure to discuss this issue, a failure to introspect, means a lost historical opportunity. It means the failure of a radical possibility. Content with blaming European incursions, Brahmin academics are unashamedly silent about the violence perpetrated by the caste system, by Sanskrit hegemony, by the misogynist regimentation of life that is central to the Hindu social order. These are the reasons why, even as I render into English a book of Tamil love poetry, I carry the battle-axe of politics with me.

The fault lines that run through society are the fault lines we see in scholarship. As verbose and pedantic as a text might be, as much as it is supported by a complex web of cross-citation, it nevertheless betrays its loyalty to its author's own class, clan, caste, race. Embarking on writing this preface, I encountered V.R. Ramachandra Dikshitar's work.[33] His reading of the *Tirukkuṟaḷ* is a reading of it alongside the Bhagavad Gita, Manusmriti and Dharmasastras. Such a reading, where he concludes that these texts reflect each other, is a perversity, a toxic muddying of the intellectual waters. He is not the first scholar to do this. The 13th-century commentator Parimēlaḻakar (yes, he of 'handsome man on the horse' fame) has been routinely called out for constructing the meaning of the *Tirukkuṟaḷ*

> in conformity with orthodox Brahmanical ideology, whereas in the view of Dravidianists, *Tirukkuṟaḷ* documents the cultural attainments of an early Tamil civilization that was free of many of the oppressive features of Indo-Aryan civilization, such as caste.[34]

It is against such a historical backdrop that we must view the efforts to liberate the *Tirukkuṟaḷ* from Brahminical appropriation.

In the face of a Hindi-centric Aryan hegemony, foregrounding Sanskrit and Brahminical traditions that upheld a patriarchal and caste-based Hindu social order, it became imperative for the Tamil intellectual and political class to reimagine and recast Tamil literature as a vehicle to assert, define and safeguard Tamil identity alongside the idea of social justice, egalitarianism and resistance to domination.[35] Because this tense history has shaped the nature of politics in Tamil society today, it doesn't need unpacking for a Tamil audience.

Of the many examples, I choose here to highlight the work of Periyar E.V. Ramasamy (1869–1972). An iconoclast and the founder of the Self-Respect movement, Periyar's ideology of rationalism, social justice, feminism and caste-annihilation awakened Tamil society and continues to form the basis for radical politics in Tamil Nadu.

On 6 November 1949, speaking at the Saidai Tiruvaḷḷuvar Manram in Chennai, Periyar declared:

> Kuṟaḷ is a text that refutes Manusmriti.
> Kuṟaḷ is a text that opposes Aryan supremacy.
> Kuṟaḷ is a text that rings the death knell for Brahminism.
> There is a necessity to spread the message of the Kuṟaḷ all over this country.[36]

Periyar attributed his praise of Tiruvaḷḷuvar to the progressive ideas espoused by the poet. Exhorting people to give up their obsession with Vaḷḷuvar's origins and birth stories, he asked them to instead focus on the message of the *Tirukkuṟaḷ*.[37] Best known for his atheism and feminism, Periyar's endorsement of the *Tirukkuṟaḷ* carried tremendous political significance. Addressing the allegation arising from his own rationalist ranks, that the *Tirukkuṟaḷ* begins with an explicit praise to God, Periyar contended that there is no mention of idolatry anywhere in the text, pointing out that in the same chapter supposedly dedicated to the worship of God, Tiruvaḷḷuvar dwells on the importance of becoming a better human being. Periyar also noted that in the following chapter – in praise of rain – Vaḷḷuvar does not hold the Hindu view that people's good conduct causes rain to fall. On the contrary, he posits that unless rain falls according to agricultural need, society would collapse and it would become impossible for people to uphold morality in the first place. This inversion, according to Periyar, is what sets apart Vaḻḻuvar as a rationalist. He also wrote:

> Tiruvaḻḻuvar's era was not one of Communism or Socialism. However, Valluvar comes across as an exceptional communist, and hence deserving of our praise.[38]

Periyar stood for a rationalist, feminist, anti-caste, emancipatory politics, and his advocacy of the *Tirukkuṟaḷ* instantly catapulted the text into the centre of radical Tamil identity.

It is worth noting that, to this day, the Brahminical urge to claim this text for itself, to subsume it as some kind of subsidiary or franchise under the Vedic tradition, has not gone away. Just a few years ago, there was a war of words between senior Dravidian politician M.K. Stalin (now Chief Minister of Tamil Nadu) and Brahmin archaeologist R. Nagaswamy, over the latter's assertions that the *Tirukkuṟaḷ* originated from the Sanskrit Vedas.[39] To bolster his case, Nagaswamy even brazenly cited sources that vehemently denied the Sanskrit-sourced theory.[40] For spectators who know the history of Tamil politics, the feeling is of being stuck in a time-loop.

A little detour here as we deconstruct Periyar's relationship to the *Tirukkuṟaḷ*. In the 1940s, he propagated the text as a Tamil counter to Hindu–Indian hegemony – a fresh bulwark against assimilation and erasure, articulating a fiercely independent identity and a way of life based on egalitarianism. In that cultural warfare, Periyar pitted text against text, language against language, a democratic culture against an oppressive one. However, Periyar did not simply stumble, unquestioning, upon the *Tirukkuṟaḷ* in the middle of his public career. In the 1920s, when he had just started formulating his early feminist ideas, he criticised the *Tirukkuṟaḷ*, alleging that 'extreme slavishness and inferiority' had been introduced in the chapters on the Worth of a Life Partner (6) and in the cautionary chapter in statecraft against Being Led by Women (91). Faced with any argument seeking to justify these sections, Periyar would ask 'if Tiruvaḷḷuvar had not been a man, but a woman who had written such kuṟaḷ, would (s)he have portrayed such ideas?'[41]

Like all our favourite writers, Tiruvaḷḷuvar can be problematic. In the text's 1330 couplets, he slips up a few times. A wife who doesn't worship God, but worships her husband? Ufff. There goes the sixth chapter. Another chapter (91) articulates collective male fears of becoming hen-pecked husbands and emasculated men, while chapter 92 rails against prostitution. This is the part of the introduction, then, where we explain away our disappointment by saying that, as much as Tiruvaḷḷuvar was a man ahead of his times, he was inevitably a product of them too. This is also where I sneak in a caveat, or two, or three. Since we are accustomed to comparing secular Tamil texts to their Brahminical–Sanskrit counterparts, my first caveat is that control of women – the classic paradigm of Sanatana Dharma – forms no part of the *Tirukkuṟaḷ*. As a feminist, I want to cite Kuṟaḷ 57, from the sixth chapter:

சிறைகாக்கும் காப்புஎவன் செய்யும் மகளிர்
நிறைகாக்கும் காப்பே தலை

ciṟaikākkum kāppevaṉ ceyyum makaḷir
niṟaikākkum kāppē talai

A rough translation would amount to:

> What is the point of prison-like vigilance?
> A woman protecting herself is the greatest safety.

Firstly: unlike Brahminical texts, the *Tirukkuṟaḷ* did not arise in a society that engaged in child marriage, where women were sequestered and given in matrimony before they even hit puberty to ensure that both their virginity and chastity was proven to the in-laws; neither does it reflect the Manuṣmriti, a supposedly divine text, which declares that all women are seductresses of whom even their fathers should be wary. While the control of women is the heartbeat of Sanatana Dharma, the Hindu social order, nowhere does the *Tirukkuṟaḷ* call for any woman to be controlled. A woman is not someone to be imprisoned, all her movements watched over – instead, she is entrusted with the task of her own protection. It is her autonomy that protects her, not her lack of it.

Secondly: unlike the Brahminical–Hindu marriage, which unites a husband and wife for seven lives, or the concept of pativrata – loyalty to a husband for eternity – the *Tirukkuṟaḷ* suggests that incompatibility can be fatal. *Don't risk your life*, is the undercurrent of this kuṟaḷ (890):

> உடம்பாடு இலாதவர் வாழ்க்கை குடங்கருள்
> பாம்போடு உடன்உறைந் தற்று
>
> *uṭampāṭu ilātavar vāḻkkai kuṭaṅkaruḷ*
> *pāmpōṭu uṭaṉuṟain taṟṟu.*

In Pope's translation:

Domestic life with those who don't agree,
Is dwelling in a shed with snake for company.

As a victim of domestic violence, I have lived through what this means – the poison of cohabiting once irreconcilable differences set in leaves no option other than certain death (of oneself, of one's identity). Vaḷḷuvar calls out the toxicity of such an arrangement, in stark opposition to the Sanatana Dharma where marriages are for life.

Thirdly: for all my misgivings over the text, I want to fundamentally distinguish between the first two parts of the *Tirukkuṟaḷ* – dealing with morality and materialism, society and statecraft – and the third, which is love poetry. Given the underlying fact that the institution of the family is of ultimate importance to the institution of the state, the first two sections demonstrate adherence to the structure of a household, the roles of husband and wife. The third part does not suffer these notions. It is a world that two lovers conjure together: gossip and social censure do not interfere with their sexual passion; instead, they feed its flames. Society does not separate the lovers; it exists outside of them. Love and sex are acts of equality and democracy – without any inherent hierarchy, they are available to everyone.

There is something special about the Iṉpattuppāl; for me, the first feminist decision was to translate this third part of the *Tirukkuṟaḷ* as a stand-alone text. When the Italian Jesuit priest Constantine Joseph Beschi (who adopted the Tamil name Vīramāmunivar) translated the *Tirukkuṟaḷ* into Latin in the 17th century, he only worked on the first two sections. The third, on love, was seen as too taboo for a Jesuit priest. Although Vīramāmunivar's work enabled European scholars of the time to encounter Tamil scholarship, his self-censorship marked the beginning of a gradual but wide-spread neglect of the *Tirukkuṟaḷ*'s third portion.

When Pope, the missionary turned scholar of Tamil, published his translations of the *Tirukkuṟaḷ* in 1886, he gave a lengthy reasoning on his decision to translate the Iṉpattuppāl. 'Something must be said regarding the Third Book on "Love",' he wrote:

> Of this Mr. Drew said, that 'it could not be translated into any European language without exposing the translator to infamy'. But this is only true in regard to certain of the commentaries upon it, which are simply detestable. I am persuaded that it is perfectly pure in its tendency, and in the intention of its wise and high-souled composer. [...] This prejudice kept me from reading the third part of the *Kurraḷ* for some years; but the idea occurred to me very forcibly that he wrote:
>
> > [மனத்துக்கண் மாசிலன் ஆதல் அனைத்தறன்
> > ஆகுல நீர பிற.
> >
> > *maṉattukkaṇ mācilaṉ ātal aṉaittaṟaṉ*
> > *ākula nīra piṟa*]
> >
> > Spotless be thou in mind! This only merits virtue's name;
> > All else, mere pomp and idle sound, no real worth can claim.
>
> [Valluvar] could not have covered himself with the spotted infamy of singing a song of lust. Thus I ventured at length to read and study it, rejecting commentators, when I was able fairly to appreciate its spirit; and, as the result, I translate it,

> believing that I shall be regarded as having done good service in doing so.[42]

In the 20th century, we see a marked shift among a section of western academics studying the *Tirukkuṟaḷ*. Shedding the characteristic Victorian repression, they single out the Iṉpattuppāl for its poetry. Kamil Zvelebil writes:

> If there is true poetry anywhere in the book it will be found among the erotic couplets of its third part, because there the teacher, the preacher in Vaḷḷuvar has stepped aside, and the poet speaks almost the language of the superb love-poetry of the classical age.[43]

Anticipating rightly that just the idea of a 'book of love' from the Indian subcontinent would be inevitably compared to the Kamasutra, he adds in a footnote:

> Here is necessary to stress that Tiruvaḷḷuvar's conception of eros is utterly different from the treatment of sex in any of the Sanskrit *kāmaśāstras*. Love, in the *Tirukkuṟaḷ* is an exalting passion pictured as ideal love in the dramatic situations according to the ancient *akam* conventions; the work of Vātsyāyana and of other Sanskrit authors is *śāstra*, that is, objective, scientific analysis of sex.

The idea of carrying a billboard-sized cautionary announcement that Tamil is NOT Sanskrit, that we are separate and we stand apart, has become a default mode of functioning for Tamil people striving to claim our rightful space and to be identified as ourselves. This necessity has touched academia too. Circling back to the uniqueness of the book of love within the *Tirukkuṟaḷ*, I want to bring in the French Tamil scholar and translator François Gros. In 1992, the prestigious Parisian publishing house Gallimard brought out his translation of 25 chapters of the *Tirukkuṟaḷ*, titled *Le Livre de l'Amour* (*The Book of Love*). It was affirming to realise that at least one translator before me had decided to approach this section of the *Tirukkuṟaḷ* as a stand-alone text, noting that it is not only the shortest but also 'the most difficult and, in certain ways, the most remarkable' of the triptych.[44]

Now that I have explained my intentions in making the third section of the *Tirukkuṟaḷ* a book in itself, let me discuss a little bit of process. I could say, like every other translator before me, that this form defies translation. Indeed, the untranslatability of the text has been noted by almost every translator, scholar and commentator to work on it. As much as every stand-alone kuṟaḷ contains a universe of meaning, they also work together as a part of the whole.[45]

My translation progressed in much the same manner that Tamil commentators of the *Tirukkuṟaḷ* have traditionally approached the work. First, through the semantic breakdown of the text's component words to explain its meaning, a process termed *padha urai* (பதவுரை) in Tamil. Referring back to the earliest commentators, the words themselves were extrapolated and tinged with regressive patriarchal meanings and interpretations. For instance, in Kuṟaḷ 1241, Parimēlaḻakar adds the contentious commentary that the woman is 'losing shame which is dearer than life' – shocking, because nowhere does Tiruvaḷḷuvar write that shame is dearer than life. While this is a good example of the impositions and infiltrations of patriarchal ideas into the text, I am writing an introduction rather than a dissertation, and will not dwell on every instance where such loaded commentaries exist. After all, the reason for undertaking a feminist translation in the first place was to break free from this hegemonic, oppressive tradition.

Parimēlaḻakar is a known offender, and while he has been sufficiently taken to task by Tamil scholars for smuggling several concepts of the Brahminical social order into the text, they have not singled him out for also foisting onto it a patriarchal outlook via his overemphasis on chastity, shame, and generalised misogyny.[46] Instead of rejecting these constructs outright, Tamil male scholars seemed to have accepted them as a given, something foundational to every society. This is an injustice that needs to be undone. So, before I embarked on my own rendering, I took the time to pause and to observe how judgemental values of reserve, Victorian morality, Brahminical patriarchy and rigid notions of masculine–feminine value systems have impregnated the existing translations. Like a circuit-breaker, this essential step ensured that these burdens did not carry over into my own translation, either subconsciously or because of deep-rooted conditioning.

Likewise, I also worked towards eliminating archaic words from translations. Often, because the men who were translating the kuṟaḷs happened to be Christian missionaries or Hindu religious reformists, there is a marked tendency of the translated text to be discreet and vague. There are many instances where sex is referred as 'union' or 'congress' in the English translation – almost as if the translators were scandalised by the idea of sex. Sulking and quarrelling (very essential to Tamil love stories) go by the word 'bouderie', which, for all its French affectation, is not readily accessible to the reader in English.

In every Tamil volume of the *Tirukkuṟaḷ* still in print, the Iṉpattuppāl is separated into two sections: kaḷaviyal (the first seven chapters) and kaṟpiyal (the remaining 18 chapters). *Kaḷavu* has often been mistranslated as denoting the clandestine meeting of lovers, with *kaṟpu* referring to the wedded (chaste) state of married life. These distinctions have been taken as a given, following the edict of Parimēlaḻakar. I have decided to forego this division, finding it reductive. François Gros describes *kaḷavu* and *kaṟpu* as 'the beacons of the Tamil literary erotic landscape', holding the spontaneity of unsanctioned love versus conjugal love in opposition to each other and writing that 'all the attraction of the former depends upon the myth of the first meeting and all the charm of the latter on reconciliation after absences or quarrels'.[47] Perhaps that is true. What is equally true is that this translation comes into being in a society where women continue to inhabit a shaming culture, where offhand divisions of premarital or clandestine love versus married love will feed damaging stereotypes. I encourage readers not to be encumbered by these internal divisions of the text; after all, they were imposed upon the *Tirukkuṟaḷ* centuries after it was originally written.

While reading English translations of the *Tirukkuṟaḷ*, I was uneasy to notice that the verses are often translated as a long, single sentence, or rendered (through the use of some force, I would like to believe) as a rhyming couplet. In my opinion, the first choice reads like someone's interior musing; the second, like a teenager's first attempt at poetry. English has the word order of Subject-Verb-Object (SVO), whereas Tamil uses Subject-Object-Verb. The main verb of a Tamil kuṟaḷ comes at the end, whereas in English it comes in the middle. This affects the translation, because, for poetry, the turn of thought, that revealing moment of comparison, is crucial. To remain true to the spirit of the original rather than its visual form, I have used four-line free-verse stanzas to capture two-line kuṟaḷs, with the line breaks helping to achieve the dénouements of its first and second halves. Remaining true to the mood of the kuṟaḷ mattered to me as a feminist – especially because a lot of the verses express female desire, and it was important to capture how it was expressed.

I would like to remind my readers that as much as the *Tirukkuṟaḷ* stands in opposition to Brahminical–Sanskrit texts which perpetuate ideas of birth-based inequality, it also stands in opposition to them through its celebration of female desire. Unlike texts that condemn women's desire, the *Tirukkuṟaḷ* presents it with no holds barred – especially notable when we compare the book to the Manusmriti's misogynist scaremongering, or to the Hindu epic Ramayana, which posits women's desire as the root of all evil.

Weeding out the smallest remnants of patriarchal, misogynist and otherwise reductive translations was crucial to my work. I can provide a multitude of examples from within the resulting text, but for the purposes of this introductory essay, let me choose the simple but contentious word *niṟai* (நிறை).

The University of Madras *Tamil Lexicon* defines the meaning in this manner:

> நிறை[3] niṟai , n. < நிறை[1]-. 1. [K. neṟe.] Completion, completeness; பூர்த்தி. நிறைப் பெருஞ் செல்வத்து நின்றக்கடைத்தும் (நாலடி, 360). 2. Fulness, repletion, copiousness, one of eight pāṭaṟ-payaṉ, q. v.; எண்வகைப் பாடற்பயன்களுள் ஒன்று.

(சிலப். 3, 16, உரை.) 3. Excellence, splendour; மாட்சிமை. வானவரேத்து நிறை கழலோன் (திருவாச. 13, 13). (சூடா.) 4. (Mus.) Note repeated often in singing a musical piece; அடுத்தடுத்துவரும் ஸ்வரம். 5. (Mus.) A time-measure consisting of two beats; இரண்டு தாக்குடைய தாளவகை. (பரிபா. 17, 18.) 6. Large water-pot; நீர்ச்சால். (சூடா.)7. The ceremony of filling up a pot with nāṭ-katir and paddy; நாட்கதிரும் நெல்லும் ஒரு பானையிலிட்டு நிறைக்கும் விசேடம். Nāñ. 8. Desire; ஆசை. (அக. நி.)

In the *Tirukkuṟaḷ*, this word occurs half a dozen times. Most often, it has been rendered by male translators as 'chastity'. Take Kuṟaḷ 1251 as an example:

காமக் கணிச்சி உடைக்கும் நிறையென்னும்
நாணுத்தாழ் வீழ்த்த கதவு.

kāmak kaṇicci uṭaikkum niṟaiyeṉṉum
nāṇuttāḻ vīḻtta katavu.

'Chastity' is not what the original text intends, and so to use it there is an imposition of post-dated cultural values on a classical text. As a poet, translator, a woman and a feminist, I wanted to avoid the burden of regressive ideas foisted onto a text that actually burns with longing, only ever concerning itself with shame in order to speak of the shame itself.

So, when my turn came to translate *niṟai* in this kuṟaḷ, I chose 'unwavering mind' – after all, *niṟai* means fullness, strength, containment. I wanted my translation to incorporate a sense of self-fulfilment, of something that does not have to wander or waver, to challenge the lazy patriarchal notion that women have fickle minds.

Here is my rendering of Kuṟaḷ 1251:

The battle-axe of passion
breaks down the door
of my unwavering mind,
bolted with my coyness.

Like its close cousin virginity, 'chastity' – upon which most translators have fallen back – denotes something physical, the classification of relationships as chaste or unchaste implying something situated in the woman's body. But the heroine here is caught in the whirlpool of passion, a battle-axe that breaks through to her – and as much as it is a metaphor, it is also about a mental state of being.

In my bid to create a feminist translation, I also took the decision to avoid words that have often been rendered in English as 'husband' or 'wife'. I wanted to stop burdening this text of love with a social custom whose contemporary connotations may be far removed from how they were employed in Tiruvaḷḷuvar's time. Instead, I have used the words 'man' and 'woman', and wherever possible, the gender-neutral 'lover'.

I believe that feminist translations of classical texts like this one are necessary interventions, correcting the course of what has been happening with the *Tirukkuṟaḷ* for the past several centuries. The wish to create a text that opens up the possibility of a non-binary reading of its source material has also spurred me on. Here, I'd like to share two examples:

கண்ணிறைந்த காரிகைக் காம்பேர்தோட் பேதைக்குப்
பெண்நிறைந்த நீர்மை பெரிது. (1272)

kaṇṇiṟainta kārikaik kāmpērtōṭ pētaikkup
peṇṇiṟainta nīrmai peritu

While I am not inclined to impose our worldview where it does not belong, I do want to allow the text to exist in and stay receptive to our times. It is true that most of the *Tirukkuṟaḷ* could be marked by (assumed) cis-heteronormativity, where an address to a male lover is read as coming from a female voice and vice versa. But how does a translator seek avenue for redress? Let us look at this phrase: *peṇṇiṟainta nīrmai peritu.*

Peṇṇiṟainta: The women-filled *nīrmai*, a *nīrmai* full of femininity
Peritu: is great, adds something, is special
Peṇṇiṟainta nīrmai
Niṟai and *nīrmai* are interrelated
Niṟainta (that filled with)
Nīrmai (the state of being filled, complete)

As for *nīrmai,* most translators have defaulted to its meaning of 'inherent nature' or 'essential quality'. However, *nīrmai* for me is not a word so much as an opportunity. *Nīrmai* comes from *nīr* (water, fluids), and could denote the property of water, and hence, liquidity, fluidity.

Therefore, I rendered this kuṟaḷ as follows:

Sleek-boned like bamboo,
this young woman is a beauty
to behold – the most remarkable
is her feminine fluidity.

To me, this seemed like a word worth being precious about. ‘Fluidity’ allows us to realise *nīrmai* as a state of flux, but also one which opens up femininity as something which can be claimed rather than something prescribed or rigid.

Let me finish with one last example of how words can be occupied in service of a broader, more inclusive politics.

> பெண்ணியலார் எல்லாரும் கண்ணின் பொதுஉண்பர்
> நண்ணேன் பரத்தநின் மார்பு. (1311)
>
> *peṇṇiyalār ellārum kaṇṇin̲ potu’uṇpar*
> *naṇṇēn̲ parattanin̲ mārpu*

Peṇṇiyalār ellārum has been translated as ‘all women’ – because of the word-root *penn*, meaning woman, but also because of the way the metreme is constructed per the rules of the venpa. But the words *peṇṇiyalār ellārum* are slightly more complexly constructed in the Tamil, bringing the meaning closer to ‘everyone who is womanlike/feminine’ and opening the kuṟaḷ to the possibility of being translated in this manner:

> Everyone with womanness
> publicly feasts their eyes—
> but I will not embrace—
> your debauched chest.

Here, the beholders are not people of a particular gender, but people of a particular inclination. At this sort of crucial juncture, it is important to bear in mind that, as a radical act of social transformation, translation can accommodate a world outside strictly defined gender roles. While it may not amount to much, knowing that I could negotiate space for an inclusive world – especially in the world of love and while staying true to the original text – was deeply gratifying to me.

The act of translating the love poetry of the *Tirukkuṟaḷ* has reinforced my belief that we need to weaponise the words we choose. In these pages, I have taken up the task of translation as interpretation. I have sought to recast translation as an act of feminist commentary, of reclaiming female desire, and of urgent, necessary subversion.

This text has lived with me for the last two decades. I go to this text whenever I am in love. As a poet, being in love has been my permanent state of being. I invite you, dear reader, to enter this beautiful world. I invite you to fall in love.

தகையணங்குறுததல்

Her Dangerous Beauty

1081. அணங்குகொல் ஆய்மயில் கொல்லோ கனங்குழை
மாதர்கொல் மாலும்என் நெஞ்சு.

aṇaṅkukol āymayil kollō kaṉaṅkuḻai
mātarkol mālum eṉ neñcu

1082. நோக்கினாள் நோக்கெதிர் நோக்குதல் தாக்கணங்கு
தானைக்கொண் டன்ன துடைத்து.

nōkkiṉāḷ nōkketir nōkkutal tākkaṇaṅku
tāṉaikkoṇ ṭaṉṉa tuṭaittu

1083. பண்டறியேன் கூற்றென் பதனை இனியறிந்தேன்
பெண்டகையால் பேரமர்க் கட்டு.

paṇṭaṟiyēṉ kūṟṟeṉ pataṉai iṉiyaṟintēṉ
peṇṭakaiyāl pēramark kaṭṭu

1084. கண்டார் உயிருண்ணும் தோற்றத்தால் பெண்டகைப்
பேதைக்கு அமர்த்தன கண்.

kaṇṭār uyiruṇṇum tōṟṟattāl peṇṭakaip
pētaikku amarttaṉa kaṇ

1085. கூற்றமோ கண்ணோ பிணையோ மடவரல்
நோக்கமிம் மூன்றும் உடைத்து.

kūṟṟamō kaṇṇō piṇaiyō maṭavaral
nōkkamim mūṉṟum uṭaittu

1081. My heart is tossed about:
is she the lusty she-devil,
a flamboyant peacock,
lady of heavy earrings?

1082. She looks, her look
a face-off to mine—
Looks like she has brought along
a shock troop of terrifying goddesses.

1083. Once, I never knew of that
which is called Death. Now
I know. It wages war with
a woman's striking eyes.

1084. Harmless, this woman,
with eyes devouring
the lives of those
who look at her.

1085. Is it ruinous death,
is it an eye, or a doe?
A woman's glance
is all of the above.

1086. கொடும்புருவம் கோடா மறைப்பின் நடுங்கஞர்
செய்யல மன்இவள் கண்.

koṭumpuruvam kōṭā maṟaippiṉ naṭuṅkañar
ceyyala maṉival kaṇ

1087. கடாஅக் களிற்றின்மேற் கட்படாம் மாதர்
படாஅ முலைமேல் துகில்.

kaṭā'ak kaḷiṟṟiṉmēṟ kaṭpaṭām mātar
paṭā'a mulaimēl tukil

1088. ஒண்ணுதற் கோஒ உடைந்ததே ஞாட்பினுள்
நண்ணாரும் உட்குமென் பீடு.

oṇṇutaṟ kō'o uṭaintatē ñāṭpiṉuḷ
naṇṇārum uṭkumeṉ pīṭu

1089. பிணையேர் மடநோக்கும் நாணும் உடையாட்கு
அணியெவனோ ஏதில தந்து.

piṇaiyēr maṭanōkkum nāṇum uṭaiyāṭku
aṇiyevaṉō ētila tantu

1090. உண்டார்கண் அல்லது அடுநறாக் காமம்போல்
கண்டார் மகிழ்செய்தல் இன்று.

uṇṭārkaṇ allatu aṭunaṟāk kāmampōl
kaṇṭār makiḻceytal iṉṟu

1086. If those cruel eyebrows,
unlined, would hide her eyes –
her eyes would not make me
shiver in this manner.

1087. This fine garment, not touching
this woman's breasts, ornamental,
as the blindfold over a male
elephant, raging in mast.

1088. My legendary valour
made foes tremble,
now it lies shattered
seeing her lustrous brow.

1089. Doe-eyed and bashful,
she casts a guileless look.
Does she need these jewels?
They run alien to her nature.

1090. Distilled liquor causes no delight
to those who are not drunk,
unlike love that intoxicates
at a mere glimpse.

குறிப்பறிதல்

The Signs of Attraction

1091. இருநோக்கு இவளுண்கண் உள்ளது ஒருநோக்கு
நோய்நோக்கொன் றந்நோய் மருந்து.

irunōkku ivaḷuṇkaṇ uḷḷatu orunōkku
nōynōkkoṉ ṟannōy maruntu

1092. கண்களவு கொள்ளும் சிறுநோக்கம் காமத்தில்
செம்பாகம் அன்று பெரிது.

kaṇkaḷavu koḷḷum ciṟunōkkam kāmattil
cempākam aṉṟu peritu

1093. நோக்கினாள் நோக்கி இறைஞ்சினாள் அஃதவள்
யாப்பினுள் அட்டிய நீர்.

nōkkiṉāḷ nōkki iṟaiñciṉāḷ aḥtavaḷ
yāppiṉuḷ aṭṭiya nīr

1094. யான்நோக்கும் காலை நிலன்நோக்கும் நோக்காக்கால்
தான்நோக்கி மெல்ல நகும்.

yāṉnōkkum kālai nilaṉnōkkum nōkkākkāl
tāṉnōkki mella nakum

1095. குறிக்கொண்டு நோக்காமை அல்லால் ஒருகண்
சிறக்கணித்தாள் போல நகும்

kuṟikkoṇṭu nōkkāmai allāl orukaṇ
ciṟakkaṇittāḷ pōla nakum

1091. Her eyes hold two glances.
One, the glance that causes
this disease, and two,
the medicine that cures.

1092. A little
stolen glance
is so much more
than so much sex.

1093. She looked,
looking gushed forth—
These, the currents, the cascades
in the grammars of our love.

1094. While I look at her,
she gazes at the ground.
While I look away,
she looks at me, smiling.

1095. She avoids looking
straight at me – she casts
her side-long glances
and smiles.

1096. உறாஅ தவர்போல் சொலினும் செறாஅர்சொல்
ஒல்லை உணரப் படும்.

kuṟikkoṇṭu nōkkāmai allāl orukaṇ
ciṟakkaṇittāḷ pōla nakum

1097. செறாஅச் சிறுசொல்லும் செற்றார்போல் நோக்கும்
உறாஅர்போன்று உற்றார் குறிப்பு.

ceṟā'ac ciṟucollum ceṟṟārpōl nōkkum
uṟā'arpōṉṟu uṟṟār kuṟippu

1098. அசையியற்கு உண்டாண்டோர் ஏஎர்யான் நோக்கப்
பசையினள் பைய நகும்.

acaiyiyaṟku uṇṭāṇṭōr ē'eryāṉ nōkkap
pacaiyiṉaḷ paiya nakum

1099. ஏதிலார் போலப் பொதுநோக்கு நோக்குதல்
காதலார் கண்ணே உள.

ētilār pōlap potunōkku nōkkutal
kātalār kaṇṇē uḷa

1100. கண்ணொடு கண்ணிணை நோக்கொக்கின் வாய்ச்சொற்கள்
என்ன பயனும் இல.

kaṇṇoṭu kaṇiṇai nōkkokkiṉ vāyccoṟkaḷ
eṉṉa payaṉum ila

1096. Though they converse
as if they were strangers,
the words of lovers
are quickly known.

1097. Little words of anger,
looks of sworn enmity –
such deliberate indifference
is the sign of intimacy.

1098. I look at her, she melts
and gently smiles,
such bewitching charm
descends on my agile beauty.

1099. Only the eyes of lovers
are capable of glancing
the defiant public stare
of weapon-bearing foes.

1100. Eyes meeting
to hold a gaze
render all talk
useless.

புணர்ச்சிமகிழ்தல்

The Pleasure of Sex

1101. கண்டுகேட்டு உண்டுயிர்த்து உற்றறியும் ஐம்புலனும்
ஒண்தொடி கண்ணே உள.

kaṇṭukēṭṭu uṇṭuyirttu uṟṟaṟiyum aimpulaṉum
oṇtoṭi kaṇṇē uḷa

1102. பிணிக்கு மருந்து பிறமன் அணியிழை
தன்நோய்க்குத் தானே மருந்து.

piṇikku maruntu piṟamaṉ aṇiyiḻai
taṉṉōykkut tāṉē maruntu

1103. தாம்வீழ்வார் மென்றோள் துயிலின் இனிதுகொல்
தாமரைக் கண்ணான் உலகு.

tāmvīḻvār meṉṟōḷ tuyiliṉ iṉitukol
tāmaraik kaṇṇāṉ ulaku

1104. நீங்கின் தெறூஉம் குறுகுங்கால் தண்ணென்னும்
தீயாண்டுப் பெற்றாள் இவள்.

nīṅkiṉ teṟū'um kuṟukuṅkāl taṇṇeṉṉum
tīyāṇṭup peṟṟāḷ ivaḷ

1105. வேட்ட பொழுதின் அவையவை போலுமே
தோட்டார் கதுப்பினாள் தோள்.

vēṭṭa poḻutiṉ avaiyavai
pōlumē tōṭ ṭār katuppiṉāḷ tōḷ

1101. To look, to hear, to taste,
to smell, to touch:
all my five senses enjoy
the presence of this bangled beauty.

1102. Cure for ailments
are found elsewhere:
for the disease she causes
she alone is the cure.

1103. Even the world
of the lotus-eyed lord
is not as sweet as sleep
in the soft arms of my beloved.

1104. If I move away, it burns,
if I come closer, it cools—
Where did she
get this fire?

1105. Whatever I wish
is granted that very instant
by this beautiful woman
wearing flowers in her hair.

1106. உறுதோறு உயிர்தளிர்ப்பத் தீண்டலால் பேதைக்கு
அமிழ்தின் இயன்றன தோள்.

uṟutōṟu uyirtaḷirppat tīṇṭalāl pētaikku
amiḻtiṉ iyaṉṟaṉa tōḷ

1107. தம்மில் இருந்து தமதுபாத்து உண்டற்றால்
அம்மா அரிவை முயக்கு.

tam'mil iruntu tamatupāttu uṇṭaṟṟāl
am'mā arivai muyakku

1108. வீழும் இருவர்க்கு இனிதே வளியிடை
போழப் படாஅ முயக்கு.

vīḻum iruvarkku iṉitē vaḷiyiṭai
pōḻap paṭā'a muyakku

1109. ஊடல் உணர்தல் புணர்தல் இவைகாமம்
கூடியார் பெற்ற பயன்.

ūṭal uṇartal puṇartal ivaikāmam
kūṭiyār peṟṟa payaṉ

1110. அறிதோறு அறியாமை கண்டற்றால் காமம்
செறிதோறும் சேயிழை மாட்டு.

aṟitōṟu aṟiyāmai kaṇṭaṟṟāl kāmam
ceṟitōṟum cēyiḻai māṭṭu

1106. Every embrace
breathes fresh life
into me; her body
is sweetest nectar.

1107. In the embrace
of this black beauty:
the intimacy of home,
the comfort of a family meal.

1108. Lovers treasure being locked
in an embrace that does not allow
even the smallest intrusion
by the gentlest breeze.

1109. Quarrel.
Reconcile.
Make love.
These, the lovers' rewards.

1110. Through learning, one sees
what one did not know.
Through sex, the jewelled
woman gets hooked.

நலம்புனைந்துரைத்தல்

In Praise of Her Beauty

1111. நன்னீரை வாழி அனிச்சமே நின்னினும்
மென்னீரள் யாம்வீழ் பவள்.

naṉṉīrai vāḻi aṉiccamē niṉṉiṉum
meṉṉīraḷ yāmvīḻ paval

1112. மலர்காணின் மையாத்தி நெஞ்சே இவள்கண்
பலர்காணும் பூவொக்கும் என்று.

malarkāṇiṉ maiyātti neñcē ivaḷkaṇ
palarkāṇum pūvokkum eṉṟu

1113. முறிமேனி முத்தம் முறுவல் வெறிநாற்றம்
வேலுண்கண் வேய்த்தோ ளவட்கு.

muṟimēṉi muttam muṟuval veṟināṟṟam
vēluṇkaṇ vēyttō ḷavaṭku

1114. காணின் குவளை கவிழ்ந்து நிலன்நோக்கும்
மாணிழை கண்ணொவ்வேம் என்று.

kāṇiṉ kuvaḷai kaviḻntu nilaṉnōkkum
māṇiḻai kaṇṇovvēm eṉṟu

1115. அனிச்சப்பூக் கால்களையாள் பெய்தாள் நுசுப்பிற்கு
நல்ல படாஅ பறை

aṉiccappūk kālkaḷaiyāḷ peytāḷ nucuppiṟku
nalla paṭā'a paṟai

1111. May you live long and prosper,
most delicate aniccham flower!
That woman I love
is even more tender!

1112. Oh heart, melting
at the mere sight of flowers,
you compare her eyes to them.
(Ah, what common taste!)

1113. My bamboo-shouldered beauty has
a slender frame, a pearly smile,
a fragrance that drives me wild,
and eyes that pierce like lances.

1114. If it could see her, the blue water lily
would fall over, hang its head in shame,
and say: I can never be a match to the eyes
of this beautiful, bejewelled woman.

1115. She wears aniccham flowers
with their stem intact –
no parai drumbeats will
cheer her (breaking) waist.

1116. மதியும் மடந்தை முகனும் அறியா
பதியின் கலங்கிய மீன்.

matiyum maṭantai mukaṉum aṟiyā
patiyiṉ kalaṅkiya mīṉ

1117. அறுவாய் நிறைந்த அவிர்மதிக்குப் போல
மறுவுண்டோ மாதர் முகத்து.

aṟuvāy niṟainta avirmatikkup pōla
maṟuvuṇṭō mātar mukattu

1118. மாதர் முகம்போல் ஒளிவிட வல்லையேல்
காதலை வாழி மதி.

mātar mukampōl oḷiviṭa vallaiyēl
kātalai vāḻi mati

1119. மலரன்ன கண்ணாள் முகமொத்தி யாயின்
பலர்காணத் தோன்றல் மதி.

malaraṉṉa kaṇṇāḷ mukamotti yāyiṉ
palarkāṇat tōṉṟal mati

1120. அனிச்சமும் அன்னத்தின் தூவியும் மாதர்
அடிக்கு நெருஞ்சிப் பழம்.

aṉiccamum aṉṉattiṉ tūviyum mātar
aṭikku neruñcip paḻam

1116. Transfixed, shaken up,
the stars sink into confusion,
not knowing how to discern
a full moon from my woman's face.

1117. Are there blots
on my woman's face
like the glowing moon
that changes phase?

1118. If you have the power
to shine like my woman's face –
live long and prosper, dear moon.
You too shall have some of my love!

1119. If your face
can hold up
against my flower-eyed lady
then rise and shine, dear moon.

1120. Aniccham, delicate flower,
drooping upon touch, or breath,
and even swan feathers are,
to her feet, thorny nerunchi.

காதற்சிறப்புரைத்தல்

In Praise of Love

1121. பாலொடு தேன்கலந் தற்றே பணிமொழி
வாலெயிறு ஊறிய நீர்.

pāloṭu tē̱ṉkalan ta̱ṟṟē paṇimoḻi
vāleyiṟu ūṟiya nīr

1122. உடம்பொடு உயிரிடை என்னமற் றன்ன
மடந்தையொடு எம்மிடை நட்பு.

uṭampoṭu uyiriṭai eṉṉamaṟ ṟaṉṉa
maṭantaiyoṭu em'miṭai naṭpu

1123. கருமணியிற் பாவாய்நீ போதாய்யாம் வீழும்
திருநுதற்கு இல்லை இடம்.

karumaṇiyiṟ pāvāynī pōtāyyām vīḻum
tirunutaṟku illai iṭam

1124. வாழ்தல் உயிர்க்கன்னள் ஆயிழை சாதல்
அதற்கன்னள் நீங்கு மிடத்து.

vāḻtal uyirkkaṉṉaḷ āyiḻai cātal
ataṟkaṉṉaḷ nīṅkum iṭattu

1125. உள்ளுவன் மன்யான் மறப்பின் மறப்பறியேன்
ஒள்ளமர்க் கண்ணாள் குணம்.

uḷḷuvaṉ maṉyāṉ maṟappiṉ maṟappaṟiyēṉ
oḷḷamark kaṇṇāḷ kuṇam

1121. Sweet of speech,
her voice is husky dew—
Her lingering kisses
are milk and honey.

1122. Whatever it is between
body and life, nothing else
lies in the friendship between
this woman and me.

1123. Get away, image
in my pupil. My beloved
with the beautiful forehead
needs more space.

1124. My dazzling beloved
in my life, I feel alive.
Where she moves away
from me, death comes.

1125. I would think of her
if I were to forget her.
How could I forget the one
with battle-ready eyes?

1126. கண்ணுள்ளின் போகார் இமைப்பின் பருவரார்
நுண்ணியர்எங் காத லவர்.

kaṇṇuḷḷiṉ pōkār imaippiṉ paruvarār
nuṇṇiyar'eṅ kāta lavar

1127. கண்ணுள்ளார் காத லவராகக் கண்ணும்
எழுதேம் கரப்பாக்கு அறிந்து.

kaṇṇuḷḷār kāta lavarākak kaṇṇum
eḻutēm karappākku aṟintu

1128. நெஞ்சத்தார் காத லவராக வெய்துண்டல்
அஞ்சுதும் வேபாக் கறிந்து.

neñcattār kāta lavarāka veytuṇṭal
añcutum vēpāk kaṟintu

1129. இமைப்பின் கரப்பாக்கு அறிவல் அனைத்திற்கே
ஏதிலர் என்னும்இவ் வூர்.

imaippiṉ karappākku aṟival aṉaittiṟkē
ētilar eṉṉumiv vūr

1130. உவந்துறைவர் உள்ளத்துள் என்றும் இகந்துறைவர்
ஏதிலர் என்னும்இவ் வூர்.

uvantuṟaivar uḷḷattuḷ eṉṟum ikantuṟaivar
ētilar eṉṉumiv vūr

1126. My eyes, he does not leave,
nor feels pain, were I to blink—
My incredible lover moves
in the most minute ways.

1127. Because inside these eyes
my lover resides, and because
I've known the hidden is stolen,
I do not write even my eyes.

1128. Inside my heart,
my lover dwells.
I fear eating hot food
for he could be scalded.

1129. I know that if I blink my eyes,
my lover might go missing – so
(for my sleeplessness), this village
considers him a cruel foe.

1130. He lives in my heart,
forever, and joyously.
This village calls him
the stranger who lives apart.

நாணுத்துறவுரைத்தல்

Renouncing Shame

1131. காமம் உழந்து வருந்தினார்க்கு ஏமம்
மடலல்லது இல்லை வலி.

kāmam uḻantu varuntiṉārkku ēmam
maṭalallatu illai vali

1132. நோனா உடம்பும் உயிரும் மடலேறும்
நாணினை நீக்கி நிறுத்து.

nōṉā uṭampum uyirum maṭalēṟum
nāṇiṉai nīkki niṟuttu

1133. நாணொடு நல்லாண்மை பண்டுடையேன் இன்றுடையேன்
காமுற்றார் ஏறும் மடல்.

nāṇoṭu nallāṇmai paṇṭuṭaiyēṉ iṉṟuṭaiyēṉ
kāmuṟṟār ēṟum maṭal

1134. காமக் கடும்புனல் உய்க்குமே நாணொடு
நல்லாண்மை என்னும் புணை.

kāmak kaṭumpuṉal uykkumē nāṇoṭu
nallāṇmai eṉṉum puṇai

1135. தொடலைக் குறுந்தொடி தந்தாள் மடலொடு
மாலை உழக்கும் துயர்.

toṭalaik kuṟuntoṭi tantāḷ maṭaloṭu
mālai uḻakkum tuyar

1131. There is no other way
than riding the madal
for those (now) broken with longing
having (once) enjoyed sexual pleasure.

1132. Throw away shame
and mount the madal—
My body and soul cannot endure
any more suffering.

1133. In another time,
I had a sense of shame,
and strength of mind—
Today, only the madal of the lovelorn.

1134. The fierce flood of lust
has washed away
the rafts of shame
and self-control.

1135. This woman wearing
tiny garland-like bracelets
gifted me the madal,
the lovesickness of evenings.

1136. மடலூர்தல் யாமத்தும் உள்ளுவேன் மன்ற
படல்ஒல்லா பேதைக்கென் கண்.

maṭalūrtal yāmattum uḷḷuvēṉ maṉṟa
paṭalollā pētaikkeṉ kaṇ

1137. கடலன்ன காமம் உழந்தும் மடலேறாப்
பெண்ணின் பெருந்தக்க தில்.

kaṭalaṉṉa kāmam uḻantum maṭalēṟāp
peṇṇiṉ peruntakka til

1138. நிறையரியர் மன்அளியர் என்னாது காமம்
மறையிறந்து மன்று படும்.

niṟaiyariyar maṉaḷiyar eṉṉātu kāmam
maṟaiyiṟantu maṉṟu paṭum

1139. அறிகிலார் எல்லாரும் என்றேஎன் காமம்
மறுகின் மறுகும் மருண்டு.

aṟikilār ellārum eṉṟē'eṉ kāmam
maṟukiṉ maṟukum maruṇṭu

1140. யாம்கண்ணின் காண நகுப அறிவில்லார்
யாம்பட்ட தாம்படா ஆறு.

yāmkaṇṇiṉ kāṇa nakupa aṟivillār
yāmpaṭṭa tāmpaṭā āṟu

1136. Even at midnight hour
I deliberate riding the madal—
I am sleepless, my eyes
restlessly seek her.

1137. There is nothing more majestic
than the woman who refuses
to ride the madal, though she
has desires vast as oceans.

1138. 'This person lacks self-control',
'This person deserves great love'—
Desire does not weigh such thoughts.
Even when hidden, it manifests publicly.

1139. Worried that no one
knows of its existence,
my desire defends itself
by taking to the streets.

1140. They mock me
to my face –
the fools who have
never undergone what I have.

அலரறிவுறுத்தல்

Lessons from Gossip

1141. அலரெழ ஆருயிர் நிற்கும் அதனைப்
பலரறியார் பாக்கியத் தால்.

alarel̲a āruyir nir̲kum atan̲aip
palarar̲iyār pākkiyat tāl

1142. மலரன்ன கண்ணாள் அருமை அறியாது
அலரெமக்கு ஈந்ததிவ் வூர்.

malaran̲n̲a kaṇṇāḷ arumai ar̲iyātu
alaremakku īntativ vūr

1143. உறாஅதோ ஊரறிந்த கௌவை அதனைப்
பெறாஅது பெற்றன்ன நீர்த்து.

ur̲ā'atō ūrar̲inta keḷavai atan̲aip
per̲ā'atu per̲r̲an̲n̲a nīrttu

1144. கவ்வையால் கவ்விது காமம் அதுவின்றேல்
தவ்வென்னும் தன்மை இழந்து.

kavvaiyāl kavvitu kāmam atuvin̲r̲ēl
tavven̲n̲um tan̲mai il̲antu

1145. களித்தொறும் கள்ளுண்டல் வேட்டற்றால் காமம்
வெளிப்படுந் தோறும் இனிது.

kaḷittor̲um kaḷḷuṇṭal vēṭṭar̲r̲āl kāmam
veḷippaṭun tōr̲um in̲itu

1141. Rumour sustains
my precious life –
not many know this.
We are indeed lucky!

1142. Unaware of the worth
of my flower-eyed beloved,
this village gifted me
poisonous gossip.

1143. This rumour,
this talk of the town,
makes us feel we have got
what we have not.

1144. Embroiled in scandal,
sex gets a high, turns
thrilling – else, it loses
its swag, its brag.

1145. Wine is a welcome joy
when rejoicing—
Public gossip heightens
the pleasure of sex.

1146. கண்டது மன்னும் ஒருநாள் அலர்மன்னும்
திங்களைப் பாம்புகொண் டற்று.

kaṇṭatu maṉṉum orunāḷ alarmaṉṉum
tiṅkaḷaip pāmpukoṇ ṭaṟṟu

1147. ஊரவர் கௌவை எருவாக அன்னைசொல்
நீராக நீளும்இந் நோய்.

ūravar kavvai eruvāka aṉṉaicol
nīrāka nīḷumin nō

1148. நெய்யால் எரிநுதுப்பேம் என்றற்றால் கௌவையால்
காமம் நுதுப்பேம் எனல்.

neyyāl erinutuppēm eṉṟaṟṟāl keḷavaiyāl
kāmam nutuppēm eṉal

1149. அலர்நாண ஒல்வதோ அஞ்சலோம்பு என்றார்
பலர்நாண நீத்தக் கடை.

alarnāṇa olvatō añcalōmpu eṉṟār
palarnāṇa nīttak kaṭai

1150. தாம்வேண்டின் நல்குவர் காதலர் யாம்வேண்டும்
கௌவை எடுக்கும்இவ் வூர்.

tāmvēṇṭiṉ nalkuvar kātalar yāmvēṇṭum
kavvai eṭukkumiv vūr

1146. We met just once.
But rumour eclipses:
now we are a spectacle,
a snake swallowing the moon.

1147. Manured by village rumours,
watered by mother's
words, this disease
keeps growing.

1148. A scandal
quenches desire
the way ghee
chokes a fire

1149. My lover asked me not to be afraid,
yet he left me – a public scandal.
How could these (silly) rumours
in town ever put me to shame?

1150. Town clamouring
is what we desire;
rumours will lead
my lover to consent.

பிரிவாற்றாமை

Inability to Bear Separation

1151. செல்லாமை உண்டேல் எனக்குரை மற்றுநின்
வல்வரவு வாழ்வார்க் குரை.

cellāmai uṇṭēl eṉakkurai maṟṟuniṉ
valvaravu vāḻvārk kurai

1152. இன்கண் உடைத்தவர் பார்வல் பிரிவஞ்சும்
புன்கண் உடைத்தால் புணர்வு.

iṉkaṇ uṭaittavar pārval pirivañcum
puṉkaṇ uṭaittāl puṇarvu

1153. அரிதரோ தேற்றம் அறிவுடையார் கண்ணும்
பிரிவோ ரிடத்துண்மை யான்.

aritarō tēṟṟam aṟivuṭaiyār kaṇṇum
pirivō riṭattuṇmai yāṉ

1154. அளித்தஞ்சல் என்றவர் நீப்பின் தெளித்தசொல்
தேறியார்க்கு உண்டோ தவறு.

aḷittañcal eṉṟavar nīppiṉ teḷittacol
tēṟiyārkku uṇṭō tavaṟu

1155. ஓம்பின் அமைந்தார் பிரிவோம்பல் மற்றவர்
நீங்கின் அரிதால் புணர்வு.

ōmpiṉ amaintār pirivōmpal maṟṟavar
nīṅkiṉ aritāl puṇarvu

1151. Tell me, only if you plan
to never leave. That news
of your safe return, save it
for those who can stay alive.

1152. Just his gaze would fill me
with such pleasure; now,
the fear of a looming separation
taints even sex with sorrow.

1153. Even the wise ones hold
that it is rare to find solace
in separation – when a lover
parts, could there be staying true?

1154. He made love, he bade me
to be fearless – if he leaves
now, is it my fault for trusting
all his words of reassurance?

1155. If guard one must,
guard against his parting –
for if he leaves, getting
back together is impossible.

1156. பிரிவுரைக்கும் வன்கண்ணர் ராயின் அரிதவர்
நல்குவர் என்னும் நசை.

pirivuraikkum vaṉkaṇṇar āyiṉ aritavar
nalkuvar eṉṉum nacai

1157. துறைவன் துறந்தமை தூற்றாகொல் முன்கை
இறைஇறவா நின்ற வளை.

tuṟaivaṉ tuṟantamai tūṟṟākol muṉkai
iṟai'iṟavā niṉṟa vaḷai

1158. இன்னாது இனன்இல்ஊர் வாழ்தல் அதனினும்
இன்னாது இனியார்ப் பிரிவு.

iṉṉātu iṉaṉilūr vāḻtal ataṉiṉum
iṉṉātu iṉiyārp pirivu

1159. தொடிற்சுடின் அல்லது காமநோய் போல
விடிற்சுடல் ஆற்றுமோ தீ.

toṭiṟcuṭiṉ allatu kāmanōy pōla
viṭiṟcuṭal āṟṟumō tī

1160. அரிதாற்றி அல்லல்நோய் நீக்கிப் பிரிவாற்றிப்
பின்இருந்து வாழ்வார் பலர்.

aritāṟṟi allalnōy nīkkip pirivāṟṟip
piṉiruntu vāḻvār palar

1156. He is so cruel,
he tells me he is leaving.
And yet, I feel special
that he is in love with me.

1157. Will my bangles,
slipping from my wrists,
foretell that the renouncer
has renounced me?

1158. Life in a land with no friends
is abject misery – even
bitterer is separation
from a loved one.

1159. Lovesickness
does not burn upon touch.
Is there a fire that burns
upon separation?

1160. (Not me!) Many endure
the impossible, discard
lovesickness, survive
separation, and live on.

படர்மெலிந்திரங்கல்

A Lament of the Lovesick

1161. மறைப்பேன்மன் யானிஃதோ நோயை இறைப்பவர்க்கு
ஊற்றுநீர் போல மிகும்.

maṟaippēṉmaṉ yāṉiḥtō nōyai iṟaippavarkku
ūṟṟunīr pōla mikum

1162. கரத்தலும் ஆற்றேன்இந் நோயைநோய் செய்தார்க்கு
உரைத்தலும் நாணுத் தரும்.

karattalum āṟṟēṉin nōyainōy ceytārkku
uraittalum nāṇut tarum

1163. காமமும் நாணும் உயிர்காவாத் தூங்கும்என்
நோனா உடம்பின் அகத்து.

kāmamum nāṇum uyirkāvāt tūṅkumeṉ
nōṉā uṭampiṉ akattu

1164. காமக் கடல்மன்னும் உண்டே அதுநீந்தும்
ஏமப் புணைமன்னும் இல்.

kāmak kaṭalmaṉṉum uṇṭē atunīntum
ēmap puṇaimaṉṉum il

1165. துப்பின் எவனாவர் மன்கொல் துயர்வரவு
நட்பினுள் ஆற்று பவர்.

tuppiṉ evaṉāvar maṉkol tuyarvaravu
naṭpiṉuḷ āṟṟu pavar

1161. I would, if only I could,
hide this lovesickness—
If someone draws, it surges
forth like a gushing spring.

1162. No, I cannot conceal it.
No, I cannot explain
this disease to the man
who causes it – it is shameful!

1163. My life is torn between
lust and shame, and
this, my frail body
cannot bear.

1164. My desire is
an endless sea;
there is no raft
to swim across safely.

1165. What would be the fate
of his enemies, I wonder,
when he unleashes so much
suffering towards his friends?

1166. இன்பம் கடல்மற்றுக் காமம் அஃதடுங்கால்
துன்பம் அதனிற் பெரிது.

inpam kaṭalmar̲r̲uk kāmam aḥtaṭuṅkāl
tun̲pam atan̲ir̲ peritu

1167. காமக் கடும்புனல் நீந்திக் கரைகாணேன்
யாமத்தும் யானே உளேன்.

kāmak kaṭumpun̲al nīntik karaikāṇēn̲
yāmattum yān̲ē uḷēn̲

1168. மன்னுயிர் எல்லாம் துயிற்றி அளித்திரா
என்னல்லது இல்லை துணை.

man̲n̲uyir ellām tuyir̲r̲i aḷittirā
en̲n̲allatu illai tuṇai

1169. கொடியார் கொடுமையின் தாம்கொடிய இந்நாள்
நெடிய கழியும் இரா.

koṭiyār koṭumaiyin̲ tāmkoṭiya innāḷ
neṭiya kal̲iyum irā

1170. உள்ளம்போன்று உள்வழிச் செல்கிற்பின் வெள்ளநீர்
நீந்தல மன்னோஎன் கண்.

uḷḷampōn̲r̲u uḷval̲ic celkir̲pin̲ veḷḷanīr
nīntala man̲n̲ō'en̲ kaṇ

1166. Sex: its pleasure
(a wordless word), a sea;
its path leading to a pain
even more immense.

1167. I swim the rough seas
of sexual desire. I see
no shore – in the dead
of night, I am alone.

1168. She lulls all life on this land
to sleep – Kindest Night,
she has no one but me
to keep her company.

1169. Crueller than
my cruel one's atrocities
are these late-night hours
dragging on painfully.

1170. If, like my heart, these eyes
too could travel the inner way,
they would not have to swim
in such flooded waters.

கண்விதுப்பழிதல்

A Lament for My Eyes

1171. கண்தாம் கலுழ்வ தெவன்கொலோ தண்டாநோய்
தாம்காட்ட யாம்கண் டது.

kaṇtām kalul̲va tevan̲kolō taṇṭānōy
tāmkāṭṭa yāmkaṇ ṭatu

1172. தெரிந்துணரா நோக்கிய உண்கண் பரிந்துணராப்
பைதல் உழப்பது எவன்.

terintuṇarā nōkkiya uṇkaṇ parintuṇarāp
paital ul̲appatu evan̲

1173. கதுமெனத் தாம்நோக்கித் தாமே கலுழும்
இதுநகத் தக்க துடைத்து.

katumen̲at tāmnōkkit tāmē kalul̲um
itunakat takka tuṭaittu

1174. பெயலாற்றா நீருலந்த உண்கண் உயலாற்றா
உய்வில்நோய் என்கண் நிறுத்து.

peyalār̲r̲ā nīrulanta uṇkaṇ uyalār̲r̲ā
uyvilnōy en̲kaṇ nir̲uttu

1175. படலாற்றா பைதல் உழக்கும் கடலாற்றாக்
காமநோய் செய்தஎன் கண்.

paṭalār̲r̲ā paital ul̲akkum kaṭalār̲r̲āk
kāmanōy ceyta'en̲ kaṇ

1171. What is the reason
for such weeping, dear eyes?
You pointed out this lover to me,
who causes such incurable ache.

1172. Reckless, my eyes
looked at him—
It is pointless for them
to start grieving now.

1173. (My eyes)
they looked, they leapt into this (love),
they cry of their own accord (now) –
this is worthy of ridicule.

1174. My eyes have dried up,
they no longer shed tears,
there is no escape for me,
from this incurable disease.

1175. These eyes are plunged
in a sleepless state,
having drowned me
in a sea of lovesickness.

1176. ஓஒ இனிதே எமக்கிந்நோய் செய்தகண்
தாஅம் இதற்பட் டது.

ō'o iṉitē emakkinnōy ceytakaṇ
tā'am itaṟpaṭ ṭatu

1177. உழந்துழந் துள்நீர் அறுக விழைந்திழைந்து
வேண்டி அவர்க்கண்ட கண்.

uḻantuḻan tuḷnīr aṟuka viḻaintiḻaintu
vēṇṭi avarkkaṇṭa kaṇ

1178. பேணாது பெட்டார் உளர்மன்னோ மற்றவர்க்
காணாது அமைவில கண்.

pēṇātu peṭṭār uḷarmaṉṉō maṟṟavark
kāṇātu amaivila kaṇ

1179. வாராக்கால் துஞ்சா வரின்துஞ்சா ஆயிடை
ஆரஞர் உற்றன கண்.

vārākkāl tuñcā variṉtuñcā āyiṭai
ārañar uṟṟaṉa kaṇ

1180. மறைபெறல் ஊரார்க்கு அரிதன்றால் எம்போல்
அறைபறை கண்ணார் அகத்து.

maṟaipeṟal ūrārkku aritaṉṟāl empōl
aṟaipaṟai kaṇṇār akattu

1176. Oh, how very sweet
this poetic justice – my eyes
that inflicted this disease on me
are themselves lost in suffering!

1177. Let these eyes suffer and suffer
until all their tears dry up—
Once they had eyed him, melting
with such longing, such desire.

1178. Could there be people in love
with those who do not care
for them? My eyes have lost
their peace without seeing him.

1179. When he leaves, I'm sleepless.
When he comes, I'm sleepless.
Caught between these states,
my eyes know only sorrow.

1180. The townspeople cherish
knowing others' secrets;
but then, like drumbeats,
my eyes proclaim it all.

பசப்புறுபருவரல்

A Lament for My Skin

1181. நயந்தவர்க்கு நல்காமை நேர்ந்தேன் பசந்தவென்
பண்பியார்க்கு உரைக்கோ பிற.

nayantavarkku nalkāmai nērntēṉ pacantaveṉ
paṇpiyārkku uraikkō piṟa

1182. அவர்தந்தார் என்னும் தகையால் இவர்தந்தென்
மேனிமேல் ஊரும் பசப்பு.

avartantār eṉṉum takaiyāl ivartanteṉ
mēṉimēl ūrum pacappu

1183. சாயலும் நாணும் அவர்கொண்டார் கைம்மாறா
நோயும் பசலையும் தந்து.

cāyalum nāṇum avarkoṇṭār kaim'māṟā
nōyum pacalaiyum tantu

1184. உள்ளுவன் மன்யான் உரைப்பது அவர்திறமால்
கள்ளம் பிறவோ பசப்பு.

uḷḷuvaṉ maṉyāṉ uraippatu avartiṟamāl
kaḷḷam piṟavō pacappu

1185. உவக்காண்எம் காதலர் செல்வார் இவக்காண்என்
மேனி பசப்பூர் வது.

uvakkāṇem kātalar celvār ivakkāṇeṉ
mēṉi pacappūr vatu

1181. I blessed my lover
when he went away—
Now, to whom could I complain
about my lovesickness?

1182. Filled with pride
that he gifted it to me,
this sallowness rides me,
crawling all over my skin.

1183. Taking away my colour
and my shame, he has given
in return this lovesickness
and this sallowness of skin.

1184. He is my only thought,
his praise I sing all day long –
an intruder, this lovesick pallor
has invaded my skin.

1185. There:
my lover parts from me.
Here:
my skin turns pale.

1186. விளக்கற்றம் பார்க்கும் இருளேபோல் கொண்கன்
முயக்கற்றம் பார்க்கும் பசப்பு.

viḷakkaṟṟam pārkkum iruḷēpōl koṇkaṉ
muyakkaṟṟam pārkkum pacappu

1187. புல்லிக் கிடந்தேன் புடைபெயர்ந்தேன் அவ்வளவில்
அள்ளிக்கொள் வற்றே பசப்பு.

pullik kiṭantēṉ puṭaipeyarntēṉ avvaḷavil
aḷḷikkoḷ vaṟṟē pacappu

1188. பசந்தாள் இவள்என்பது அல்லால் இவளைத்
துறந்தார் அவர்என்பார் இல்.

pacantāḷ ivaḷeṉpatu allāl ivaḷait
tuṟantār avar'eṉpār il

1189. பசக்கமன் பட்டாங்கென் மேனி நயப்பித்தார்
நன்னிலையர் ஆவர் எனின்.

pacakkamaṉ paṭṭāṅkeṉ mēṉi nayappittār
naṉṉilaiyar āvar eṉiṉ

1190. பசப்பெனப் பேர்பெறுதல் நன்றே நயப்பித்தார்
நல்காமை தூற்றார் எனின்.

pacappeṉap pērpeṟutal naṉṟē nayappittār
nalkāmai tūṟṟār eṉiṉ

1186. Like darkness that waits
for the lamp to be put off,
this pallor waits for my man
to step out of our embrace.

1187. I was wrapped up
in his tight embrace.
I switched sides: pallor
swallowed me in that tiny gap.

1188. All of them say:
she has turned sickly pale.
None of them says:
he renounced her.

1189. Let this pallor spread
all over my skin, if only
my faraway lover
fares well.

1190. It is a fine thing to be called
a lovesick woman, as long as
they do not ruin the reputation
of the man who made me fall in love.

தனிப்படர்மிகுதி

Lament of the Lonely

1191. தாம்வீழ்வார் தம்வீழப் பெற்றவர் பெற்றாரே
காமத்துக் காழில் கனி.

tāmvīl̲vār tamvīl̲ap per̲r̲avar per̲r̲ārē
kāmattuk kāl̲il kan̲i

1192. வாழ்வார்க்கு வானம் பயந்தற்றால் வீழ்வார்க்கு
வீழ்வார் அளிக்கும் அளி.

vāl̲vārkku vān̲am payantar̲r̲āl vīl̲vārkku
vīl̲vār aḷikkum aḷi

1193. வீழுநர் வீழப் படுவார்க்கு அமையுமே
வாழுநம் என்னும் செருக்கு.

vīl̲unar vīl̲ap paṭuvārkku amaiyumē
vāl̲unam en̲n̲um cerukku.

1194. வீழப் படுவார் கெழீஇயிலர் தாம்வீழ்வார்
வீழப் படாஅர் எனின்.

vīl̲ap paṭuvār kel̲ī'iyilar tāmvīl̲vār
vīl̲ap paṭā'ar en̲in̲

1195. நாம்காதல் கொண்டார் நமக்கெவன் செய்பவோ
தாம்காதல் கொள்ளாக் கடை

nāmkātal koṇṭār namakkevan̲ ceypavō
tāmkātal koḷḷāk kaṭai

1191. Blessed are those
loved in turn by their lovers –
they enjoy the sweetest
seedless fruits of desire.

1192. The grace showered
by lovers on their beloveds
is like pouring rain
to life on earth.

1193. Those lovers,
whose love is reciprocated,
alone have the swagger to say,
'We are living the life!'

1194. Though loved (by others),
there is no deep connection
if one remains unloved
by ones own beloved.

1195. What will the one
I love do with me,
if he does not
love me back?

1196. ஒருதலையான் இன்னாது காமம்காப் போல
இருதலை யானும் இனிது.

orutalaiyāṉ iṉṉātu kāmamkāp pōla
irutalai yāṉum iṉitu

1197. பருவரலும் பைதலும் காணான்கொல் காமன்
ஒருவர்கண் நின்றொழுகு வான்.

paruvaralum paitalum kāṇāṉkol kāmaṉ
oruvarkaṇ niṉṟoḻuku vāṉ

1198. வீழ்வாரின் இன்சொல் பெறாஅது உலகத்து
வாழ்வாரின் வன்கணார் இல்.

vīḻvāriṉ iṉcol peṟā'atu ulakattu
vāḻvāriṉ vaṉkaṇār il

1199. நசைஇயார் நல்கார் எனினும் அவர்மாட்டு
இசையும் இனிய செவிக்கு.

nacai'iyār nalkār eṉiṉum avarmāṭṭu
icaiyum iṉiya cevikku

1200. உறாஅர்க்கு உறுநோய் உரைப்பாய் கடலைச்
செறாஅஅய் வாழிய நெஞ்சு.

uṟā'arkku uṟunōy uraippāy kaṭalaic
ceṟā'a'ay vāḻiya neñcu

1196. One-sided love is bitter.
Like a dancer's kavadi
poised on both shoulders,
only reciprocal love is sweet.

1197. Love-God targets
and afflicts me alone—
Does he not even notice
my sadness and longing?

1198. No one on earth
has such fortitude
as those who've never received
a kind word from the one they love.

1199. My miser of a lover
shows not deep love,
and yet, his words are
sweet music to my ears.

1200. You describe love pangs
to your unfeeling man.
Bless you, dear heart,
instead empty the sea.

நினைந்தவர்புலம்பல்

The Lament of Memory

1201. உள்ளினும் தீராப் பெருமகிழ் செய்தலால்
கள்ளினும் காமம் இனிது.

uḷḷiṉum tīrāp perumakiḻ ceytalāl
kaḷḷiṉum kāmam iṉitu

1202. எனைத்தொன்று இனிதேகாண் காமம்தாம் வீழ்வார்
நினைப்ப வருவதொன்று இல்.

eṉaittoṉṟu iṉitēkāṇ kāmamtām vīḻvār
niṉaippa varuvatoṉṟu il

1203. நினைப்பவர் போன்று நினையார்கொல் தும்மல்
சினைப்பது போன்று கெடும்.

niṉaippavar pōṉṟu niṉaiyārkol tum'mal
ciṉaippatu pōṉṟu keṭum

1204. யாமும் உளேங்கொல் அவர்நெஞ்சத்து எந்நெஞ்சத்து
ஓஒ உளரே அவர்.

yāmum uḷēṅkol avarneñcattu enneñcattu
ō'o uḷarē avar.

1205. தம்நெஞ்சத்து எம்மைக் கடிகொண்டார் நாணார்கொல்
எம்நெஞ்சத்து ஓவா வரல்.

tamneñcattu em'maik kaṭikoṇṭār nāṇārkol
emneñcattu ōvā varal

1201. Sex is sweeter than wine –
causing a ceaseless rapture
even when it is not present –
for mere memory intoxicates.

1202. Sex is sweeter
than anything else—
Mere thought of my lover
and everything else disappears

1203. He pretended to think of me
but he did not (I know).
I was about to sneeze
but I could not.

1204. Do I exist
in his heart?
Oh, he fills up
all my heart!

1205. He has a strict guard
banning my entry to his heart.
Isn't he shameless, then,
to constantly walk into mine?

1206. மற்றியான் என்னுளேன் மன்னோ அவரொடுயான்
உற்றநாள் உள்ள உளேன்.

maṟṟiyāṉ eṉṉuḷēṉ maṉṉō avaroṭuyāṉ
uṟṟanāḷ uḷḷa uḷēṉ

1207. மறப்பின் எவனாவன் மற்கொல் மறப்பறியேன்
உள்ளினும் உள்ளம் சுடும்.

maṟappiṉ evaṉāvaṉ maṟkol maṟappaṟiyēṉ
uḷḷiṉum uḷḷam cuṭum

1208. எனைத்து நினைப்பினும் காயார் அனைத்தன்றோ
காதலர் செய்யும் சிறப்பு.

eṉaittu niṉaippiṉum kāyār aṉaittaṉṟō
kātalar ceyyum ciṟappu

1209. விளியுமென் இன்னுயிர் வேறல்லம் என்பார்
அளியின்மை ஆற்ற நினைந்து.

viḷiyumeṉ iṉṉuyir vēṟallam eṉpār
aḷiyiṉmai āṟṟa niṉaintu

1210. விடாஅது சென்றாரைக் கண்ணினால் காணப்
படாஅதி வாழி மதி.

viṭā'atu ceṉṟāraik kaṇṇiṉāl kāṇap
paṭā'ati vāḻi mati

1206. I stay alive,
recollecting those days
I spent together with him.
How else could I live?

1207. What would happen
if I were to forget?
I know not forgetting;
memory burns my heart.

1208. It does not matter how
or how often I think of him –
he does not get upset.
Isn't this my lover's speciality?

1209. My dear life drains away
when I think of the heartlessness
of the man who used to say:
'We are one life.'

1210. Live long, shine on, dear moon,
until I see with my own eyes
the lover who left me, the lover
who never left my heart.

கனவுநிலையுரைத்தல்

The Solace of Dreams

1211. காதலர் தூதொடு வந்த கனவினுக்கு
யாதுசெய் வேன்கொல் விருந்து.

kātalar tūtoṭu vanta kaṉaviṉukku
yātucey vēṉkol viruntu

1212. கயலுண்கண் யானிரப்பத் துஞ்சிற் கலந்தார்க்கு
உயலுண்மை சாற்றுவேன் மன்.

kayaluṇkaṇ yāṉirappat tuñciṟ kalantārkku
uyaluṇmai cāṟṟuvēṉ maṉ

1213. நனவினால் நல்கா தவரைக் கனவினால்
காண்டலின் உண்டென் உயிர்.

naṉaviṉāl nalkā tavaraik kaṉaviṉāl
kāṇṭaliṉ uṇṭeṉ uyir

1214. கனவினான் உண்டாகும் காமம் நனவினான்
நல்காரை நாடித் தரற்கு.

kaṉaviṉāṉ uṇṭākum kāmam naṉaviṉāṉ
nalkārai nāṭit taraṟku

1215. நனவினால் கண்டதூஉம் ஆங்கே கனவுந்தான்
கண்ட பொழுதே இனிது.

naṉaviṉāl kaṇṭatū'um āṅkē kaṉavuntāṉ
kaṇṭa poḻutē iṉitu

1211. What feast shall I throw
to entertain this dream
that comes carrying
my lover's message?

1212. Fish-shaped, kohl-smudged eyes,
I plead: Proclaim the state
of my being to that man
who meets you while I sleep.

1213. Because I see in dreams
the man I cannot have
in wakefulness,
I stay alive.

1214. The sex
taking place
in my dreams fetches me
the lover I miss when I'm awake.

1215. Seeing him in my wakeful state
is indeed something—the dream, too,
is sweet the same instant
when it is seen.

1216. நனவென ஒன்றில்லை யாயின் கனவினால்
காதலர் நீங்கலர் மன்.

naṉaveṉa oṉṟillai yāyiṉ kaṉaviṉāl
kātalar nīṅkalar maṉ

1217. நனவினால் நல்காக் கொடியார் கனவினால்
என்எம்மைப் பீழிப் பது.

naṉaviṉāl nalkāk koṭiyār kaṉaviṉāl
eṉem'maip pīḻip patu

1218. துஞ்சுங்கால் தோள்மேலர் ஆகி விழிக்குங்கால்
நெஞ்சத்தர் ஆவர் விரைந்து.

tuñcuṅkāl tōḷmēlar āki viḻikkuṅkāl
neñcattar āvar viraintu

1219. நனவினால் நல்காரை நோவர் கனவினால்
காதலர்க் காணா தவர்.

naṉaviṉāl nalkārai nōvar kaṉaviṉāl
kātalark kāṇā tavar

1220. நனவினால் நம்நீத்தார் என்பர் கனவினால்
காணார்கொல் இவ்வூ ரவர்.

naṉaviṉāl namnīttār eṉpar kaṉaviṉāl
kāṇārkol ivvū ravar

1216. If there was no such thing
as waking, my lover
would never leave
in my dreams.

1217. Why does the cruel lover,
who remains unapproachable
in the waking hours, torment me
in my dreams?

1218. When I sleep, he comes
to embrace me, and as I
wake up, he hurries
and enters my heart.

1219. They fill wakefulness with
the ache of absence,
for they do not see
their lover in dreams.

1220. In reality, he abandoned her,
the people of this village say,
not being able to see
through the dreams.

பொழுதுகண்டிரங்கல்

Evening Melancholia

1221. மாலையோ அல்லை மணந்தார் உயிருண்ணும்
வேலைநீ வாழி பொழுது.

mālaiyō allai maṇantār uyiruṇṇum
vēlainī vāḻi poḻutu

1222. புன்கண்ணை வாழி மருள்மாலை எம்கேள்போல்
வன்கண்ண தோநின் துணை.

puṉkaṇṇai vāḻi maruḷmālai emkēḷpōl
vaṉkaṇṇa tōniṉ tuṇai

1223. பனிஅரும்பிப் பைதல்கொள் மாலை துனிஅரும்பித்
துன்பம் வளர வரும்.

paṉi'arumpip paitalkoḷ mālai tuṉi'arumpit
tuṉpam vaḷara varum

1224. காதலர் இல்வழி மாலை கொலைக்களத்து
ஏதிலர் போல வரும்.

kātalar ilvaḻi mālai kolaikkaḷattu
ētilar pōla varum

1225. காலைக்குச் செய்தநன்று என்கொல் எவன்கொல்யான்
மாலைக்குச் செய்த பகை.

kālaikkuc ceytanaṉṟu eṉkol evaṉkolyāṉ
mālaikkuc ceyta pakai

1221. You are not evening,
but melancholic killer-hour,
devouring married people.
Long may you live and prosper!

1222. Bless your wounded eyes,
lacklustre twilight!
Like my lover, is your
partner also cruel?

1223. Dew-laden, evening would once
tremulously make its way to me;
now, it descends in angry disgust
and makes my sorrows multiply.

1224. Lover away,
evening comes,
like a foe to the
killing fields.

1225. (Tell me)
what good have I done
to morning, and (tell me) what
wrong have I done to evening?

1226. மாலைநோய் செய்தல் மணந்தார் அகலாத
காலை அறிந்த திலேன்.

mālainōy ceytal maṇantār akalāta
kālai aṟinta tilēṉ.

1227. காலை அரும்பிப் பகலெல்லாம் போதாகி
மாலை மலரும்இந் நோய்.

kālai arumpip pakalellām pōtāki
mālai malarumin nōy

1228. அழல்போலும் மாலைக்குத் தூதாகி ஆயன்
குழல்போலும் கொல்லும் படை.

aḻalpōlum mālaikkut tūtāki āyaṉ
kuḻalpōlum kollum paṭai

1229. பதிமருண்டு பைதல் உழக்கும் மதிமருண்டு
மாலை படர்தரும் போழ்து.

patimaruṇṭu paital uḻakkum matimaruṇṭu
mālai paṭartarum pōḻtu

1230. பொருள்மாலை யாளரை உள்ளி மருள்மாலை
மாயும்என் மாயா உயிர்.

poruḷmālai yāḷarai uḷḷi maruḷmālai
māyumeṉ māyā uyir

1226. Inseparable from my spouse
in those days, I never knew
evening sickness
or what it did.

1227. Budding in the morning,
preparing to blossom all day,
this disease flowers
in the evening.

1228. Becoming a messenger
for this fire-like evening,
a killing army arrives,
as a shepherd's flute.

1229. Evening invades,
inflicting sorrow,
leaving me agitated,
making me lose my mind.

1230. Thinking of the man
given to chasing money,
my never-dying life
will die this dim evening.

உறுப்புநலனழிதல்

Wasting Away

1231. சிறுமை நமக்கொழியச் சேட்சென்றார் உள்ளி
நறுமலர் நாணின கண்.

ciṟumai namakkoḻiyac cēṭceṉṟār uḷḷi
naṟumalar nāṇiṉa kaṇ

1232. நயந்தவர் நல்காமை சொல்லுவ போலும்
பசந்து பனிவாரும் கண்.

nayantavar nalkāmai colluva pōlum
pacantu paṉivārum kaṇ

1233. தணந்தமை சால அறிவிப்ப போலும்
மணந்தநாள் வீங்கிய தோள்.

taṇantamai cāla aṟivippa pōlum
maṇantanāḷ vīṅkiya tōḷ

1234. பணைநீங்கிப் பைந்தொடி சோரும் துணைநீங்கித்
தொல்கவின் வாடிய தோள்.

paṇainīṅkip paintoṭi cōrum tuṇainīṅkit
tolkaviṉ vāṭiya tōḷ

1235. கொடியார் கொடுமை உரைக்கும் தொடியொடு
தொல்கவின் வாடிய தோள்.

koṭiyār koṭumai uraikkum toṭiyoṭu
tolkaviṉ vāṭiya tōḷ

1231. Longing for my distant lover,
my eyes shun the sight
of flowers, feeling slighted,
sad at their own demeaned state.

1232. As if to narrate
the stone-hearted nature
of my lover, my eyes
became dim and misty.

1233. These arms, so swell,
on our nuptial day –
now (wilted) proclaim
our separation.

1234. My man went away,
I withered away;
my golden bangles slide
down once-ample arms.

1235. Bearing armlets yet lacking
their old charm, these faded
shoulders narrate the cruelty
of the cruel lover.

1236. தொடியொடு தோள்நெகிழ நோவல் அவரைக்
கொடியர் எனக்கூறல் நொந்து.

toṭiyoṭu tōḷnekiḻa nōval avaraik
koṭiyar eṉakkūṟal nontu

1237. பாடு பெறுதியோ நெஞ்சே கொடியார்க்கென்
வாடுதோள் பூசல் உரைத்து.

pāṭu peṟutiyō neñcē koṭiyārkkeṉ
vāṭutōḷ pūcal uraittu

1238. முயங்கிய கைகளை ஊக்கப் பசந்தது
பைந்தொடிப் பேதை நுதல்.

muyaṅkiya kaikaḷai ūkkap pacantatu
paintoṭip pētai nutal

1239. முயக்கிடைத் தண்வளி போழப் பசப்புற்ற
பேதை பெருமழைக் கண்.

muyakkiṭait taṇvaḷi pōḻap pacappuṟṟa
pētai perumaḻaik kaṇ

1240. கண்ணின் பசப்போ பருவரல் எய்தின்றே
ஒண்ணுதல் செய்தது கண்டு.

kaṇṇiṉ pacappō paruvaral eytiṉṟē
oṇṇutal ceytatu kaṇṭu

1236. My armlets slide,
I waste away, pining—
Seeing my state, they call him
cruel, and my pain multiplies.

1237. Oh heart, glory be upon you!
Relate to that cruel one
all the clamour caused
by my drooping arms.

1238. I loosened my arms
that held her in embrace –
my beautiful, bangled woman
instantly grew pale.

1239. A gentle breeze intrudes
our tight embrace –
this young woman turns pale,
her eyes, torrential rain.

1240. Her eyes, lacking their sparkle,
went dull, and then, they saw
the state of her (once) bright
forehead, and were inconsolable.

நெஞ்சொடுகிளத்தல்

My Heart, My Traitor

1241. நினைத்தொன்று சொல்லாயோ நெஞ்சே எனைத்தொன்றும்
எவ்வநோய் தீர்க்கும் மருந்து.

niṉaittoṉṟu collāyō neñcē eṉaittoṉṟum
evvanōy tīrkkum maruntu

1242. காதல் அவரில ராகநீ நோவது
பேதைமை வாழியென் நெஞ்சு.

kātal avarila rākanī nōvatu
pētaimai vāḻiyeṉ neñcu

1243. இருந்துள்ளி என்பரிதல் நெஞ்சே பரிந்துள்ளல்
பைதல்நோய் செய்தார்கண் இல்.

iruntuḷḷi eṉparital neñcē parintuḷḷal
paitalnōy ceytārkaṇ il

1244. கண்ணும் கொளச்சேறி நெஞ்சே இவையென்னைத்
தின்னும் அவர்காணல் உற்று.

kaṇṇum koḷaccēṟi neñcē ivaiyeṉṉait
tiṉṉum avarkāṇal uṟṟu

1245. செற்றார் எனக்கை விடல்உண்டோ நெஞ்சேயாம்
உற்றால் உறாஅ தவர்.

ceṟṟār eṉakkai viṭaluṇṭō neñcēyām
uṟṟāl uṟā'a tavar

1241. Think and tell me something,
my heart, of anything,
anything that will cure
this incurable disease.

1242. When he lacks love,
it is foolishness for you
to be in pain, my dear heart –
just live long and prosper.

1243. Will sympathy come your way,
my heart, for sitting here
in lovesickness, when the one
causing this sad malady is pitiless?

1244. Take my eyes also
along with you, dear heart;
they devour me
in their longing to see him.

1245. Can we abandon him,
my heart, saying he is cruel –
this man we love
who doesn't love us?

1246. கலந்துணர்த்தும் காதலர்க் கண்டாற் புலந்துணராய்
பொய்க்காய்வு காய்திஎன் நெஞ்சு.

kalantuṇarttum kātalark kaṇṭāṟ pulantuṇarāy
poykkāyvu kāyti'eṉ neñcu

1247. காமம் விடுஒன்றோ நாண்விடு நன்னெஞ்சே
யானோ பொறேன்இவ் விரண்டு.

kāmam viṭu'oṉṟō nāṇviṭu naṉṉeñcē
yāṉō poṟēṉiv viraṇṭu

1248. பரிந்தவர் நல்காரென்று ஏங்கிப் பிரிந்தவர்
பின்செல்வாய் பேதைஎன் நெஞ்சு.

parintavar nalkāreṉṟu ēṅkip pirintavar
piṉcelvāy pētai'eṉ neñcu

1249. உள்ளத்தார் காத லவராக உள்ளிநீ
யாருழைச் சேறியென் நெஞ்சு.

uḷḷattār kāta lavarāka uḷḷinī
yāruḻaic cēṟiyeṉ neñcu

1250. துன்னாத் துறந்தாரை நெஞ்சத்து உடையேமா
இன்னும் இழத்தும் கவின்.

tuṉṉāt tuṟantārai neñcattu uṭaiyēmā
iṉṉum iḻattum kaviṉ

1246. When you meet the lover
who quells all your quarrels
by making love, my heart,
feigning slight is such a sham.

1247. Give up desire or
give up shame, good heart;
I cannot suffer
the both of them.

1248. Hoping, in his defence,
that he will show love,
my heart is a fool that follows
the man who left me.

1249. The lover resides within,
and while this is so, my heart,
who do you think about,
in search of whom do you go?

1250. He has deserted us,
he has renounced us—
If I keep him in my heart,
I will lose my beauty even more.

நிறையழிதல்

A Lament for Lost Self-Control

1251. காமக் கணிச்சி உடைக்கும் நிறையென்னும்
நாணுத்தாழ் வீழ்த்த கதவு.

kāmak kaṇicci uṭaikkum ni̱raiyeṉṉum
nāṇuttāḻ vīḻtta katavu

1252. காமம் எனவொன்றோ கண்ணின்றென் நெஞ்சத்தை
யாமத்தும் ஆளும் தொழில்.

kāmam eṉavoṉṟō kaṇṇiṉṟeṉ neñcattai
yāmattum āḷum toḻil

1253. மறைப்பேன்மன் காமத்தை யானோ குறிப்பின்றித்
தும்மல்போல் தோன்றி விடும்.

maṟaippēṉmaṉ kāmattai yāṉō kuṟippiṉṟit
tum'malpōl tōṉṟi viṭum

1254. நிறையுடையேன் என்பேன்மன் யானோஎன் காமம்
மறையிறந்து மன்று படும்.

niṟaiyuṭaiyēṉ eṉpēṉmaṉ yāṉō'eṉ kāmam
maṟaiyiṟantu maṉṟu paṭum

1255. செற்றார்பின் செல்லாப் பெருந்தகைமை காமநோய்
உற்றார் அறிவதொன்று அன்று.

ceṟṟārpiṉ cellāp peruntakaimai kāmanōy
uṟṟār aṟivatoṉṟu aṉṟu

1251. The battle-axe of passion
breaks down the door
of my unwavering mind
bolted with my coyness.

1252. What goes by the name of love
is blind, is unkind, and runs
the business of controlling
my heart even at midnight.

1253. I try and conceal
this lust of mine—
With no intimation,
it materialises like a sneeze.

1254. I am perfect, I have such
self-control, I would say,
but my hidden-away lust
betrays me, proclaiming itself publicly.

1255. Those suffering from lovesickness
shall never know the magnanimity
of not running behind those
who (now) hate us.

1256. செற்றவர் பின்சேறல் வேண்டி அளித்தரோ
எற்றென்னை உற்ற துயர்.

ceṟṟavar piṉcēṟal vēṇṭi aḷittarō
eṟṟeṉṉai uṟṟa tuyar

1257. நாணென ஒன்றோ அறியலம் காமத்தால்
பேணியார் பெட்ப செயின்.

nāṇeṉa oṉṟō aṟiyalam kāmattāl
pēṇiyār peṭpa ceyiṉ

1258. பன்மாயக் கள்வன் பணிமொழி அன்றோநம்
பெண்மை உடைக்கும் படை.

paṉmāyak kaḷvaṉ paṇimoḻi aṉṟōnam
peṇmai uṭaikkum paṭai

1259. புலப்பல் எனச்சென்றேன் புல்லினேன் நெஞ்சம்
கலத்தல் உறுவது கண்டு.

pulappal eṉacceṉṟēṉ pulliṉēṉ neñcam
kalattal uṟuvatu kaṇṭu

1260. நிணந்தீயில் இட்டன்ன நெஞ்சினார்க்கு உண்டோ
புணர்ந்தூடி நிற்பேம் எனல்.

niṇantīyil iṭṭaṉṉa neñciṉārkku uṇṭō
puṇarntūṭi niṟpēm eṉal

1256. So graceful of you,
my dearest grief,
that you run after
the one who scorns me!

1257. That something called shyness
remains a stranger
when desire drives lovers
to indulge in the excess.

1258. This sly enchanter and
his artful words, are they
not the army that breaks
into our womanness?

1259. I went, in a mood to quarrel.
I hugged him,
seeing my heart melt
for our coming together.

1260. Having just had sex,
is it possible to brood
and bicker, for these hearts
that melt like fat in fire?

அவர்வயின் விதும்பல்

Yearning

1261. வாளற்றுப் புற்கென்ற கண்ணும் அவர்சென்ற
நாளொற்றித் தேய்ந்த விரல்.

vāḷaṟṟup puṟkeṉṟa kaṇṇum avarceṉṟa
nāḷoṟṟit tēynta viral

1262. இலங்கிழாய் இன்று மறப்பின்என் தோள்மேல்
கலங்கழியும் காரிகை நீத்து.

ilaṅkiḻāy iṉṟu maṟappiṉeṉ tōḷmēl
kalaṅkaḻiyum kārikai nīttu

1263. உரன்நசைஇ உள்ளம் துணையாகச் சென்றார்
வரல்நசைஇ இன்னும் உளேன்.

uraṉnacai'i uḷḷam tuṇaiyākac ceṉṟār
varalnacai'i iṉṉum uḷēṉ

1264. கூடிய காமம் பிரிந்தார் வரவுள்ளிக்
கோடுகொ டேறுமென் நெஞ்சு.

kūṭiya kāmam pirintār varavuḷḷik
kōṭuko ṭēṟumeṉ neñcu

1265. காண்கமன் கொண்கனைக் கண்ணாரக் கண்டபின்
நீங்கும்என் மென்தோள் பசப்பு.

kāṇkamaṉ koṇkaṉaik kaṇṇārak kaṇṭapiṉ
nīṅkumeṉ meṉtōḷ pacappu

1261. I lack the light in my eyes,
they have grown dull; and,
counting the days since he left,
my fingers, too, have worn away.

1262. My dear, bejewelled, dazzling girl!
If I forget him today, these armlets
will slide off my shoulders
as I waste away...

1263. Strong-willed, my braveheart
went away to court victory—
I remain alive, longing
for his return.

1264. I think of the impending
arrival of the one who left me;
I think of all the sex we used
to have – my heart soars!

1265. I shall gaze at him
until my eyes have
had their fill – my skin's
sallowness shall go away.

1266. வருகமன் கொண்கன் ஒருநாள் பருகுவன்
பைதல்நோய் எல்லாம் கெட.

varukaman̲ koṇkan̲ orunāḷ parukuvan̲
paitalnōy ellām keṭa

1267. புலப்பேன்கொல் புல்லுவேன் கொல்லோ கலப்பேன்கொல்
கண்அன்ன கேளிர் வரின்.

pulappēn̲kol pulluvēn̲ kollō kalappēn̲kol
kaṇan̲n̲a kēḷir varin̲

1268. வினைகலந்து வென்றீக வேந்தன் மனைகலந்து
மாலை அயர்கம் விருந்து.

vin̲aikalantu ven̲r̲īka vēntan̲ man̲aikalantu
mālai ayarkam viruntu

1269. ஒருநாள் எழுநாள்போல் செல்லும்சேண் சென்றார்
வருநாள்வைத்து ஏங்கு பவர்க்கு.

orunāḷ el̲unāḷpōl cellumcēṇ cen̲r̲ār
varunāḷvaittu ēṅku pavarkku

1270. பெறின்என்னாம் பெற்றக்கால் என்னாம் உறினென்னாம்
உள்ளம் உடைந்துக்கக் கால்.

per̲in̲en̲n̲ām per̲r̲akkāl en̲n̲ām ur̲in̲en̲n̲ām
uḷḷam uṭaintukkak kāl

1266. One day, my man
will return – I shall drink,
I shall devour and enjoy him,
until all my lovesickness is destroyed.

1267. Would I quarrel, would I embrace,
would I have sex –
when the love of my life,
the light in my eyes, returns to me?

1268. Engaged in action,
may the ruler taste victory!
I shall join my woman
and feast this evening.

1269. A day passes like a week
to those who yearn the day
of return of a lover
gone faraway.

1270. What is the point of my reaching her?
What is the point of my having reached her?
What is the point of my becoming one with her?
When she is shattered by heartbreak.

குறிப்பறிவுறுத்தல்

Reading the Signs

1271. கரப்பினுங் கையிகந் தொல்லாநின் உண்கண்
உரைக்கல் உறுவதொன் றுண்டு.

karappiṉuṅ kaiyikan tollāniṉ uṇkaṇ
uraikkal uṟuvatoṉ ṟuṇṭu

1272. கண்நிறைந்த காரிகைக் காம்பேர்தோட் பேதைக்குப்
பெண்நிறைந்த நீர்மை பெரிது.

kaṇṇiṟainta kārikaik kāmpērtōṭ pētaikkup
peṇṇiṟainta nīrmai peritu

1273. மணியில் திகழ்தரு நூல்போல் மடந்தை
அணியில் திகழ்வதொன்று உண்டு.

maṇiyil tikaḻtaru nūlpōl maṭantai
aṇiyil tikaḻvatoṉṟu uṇṭu

1274. முகைமொக்குள் உள்ளது நாற்றம்போல் பேதை
நகைமொக்குள் உள்ளதொன் றுண்டு.

mukaimokkuḷ uḷḷatu nāṟṟampōl pētai
nakaimokkuḷ uḷḷatoṉ ṟuṇṭu

1275. செறிதொடி செய்திறந்த கள்ளம் உறுதுயர்
தீர்க்கும் மருந்தொன்று உடைத்து.

ceṟitoṭi ceytiṟanta kaḷḷam uṟutuyar
tīrkkum maruntoṉṟu uṭaittu

1271. Overpowering you,
your painted eyes
tell me there is something
that you are hiding.

1272. Sleek-boned like bamboo,
this young woman is a beauty
to behold – the most remarkable
is her feminine fluidity.

1273. Like glimmering thread
that holds a beaded chain,
something runs through
this woman's appeal.

1274. Like the fragrance held
within a bud, something
lies concealed within
her blossoming smile.

1275. In the hidden mischief
of my lady of many bangles,
there is a medicine to heal
heart-breaking sorrow.

1276. பெரிதாற்றிப் பெட்பக் கலத்தல் அரிதாற்றி
அன்பின்மை சூழ்வ துடைத்து.

peritāṟṟip peṭpak kalattal aritāṟṟi
aṉpiṉmai cūḻva tuṭaittu

1277. தண்ணந் துறைவன் தணந்தமை நம்மினும்
முன்னம் உணர்ந்த வளை.

taṇṇan tuṟaivaṉ taṇantamai nam'miṉum
muṉṉam uṇarnta vaḷai

1278. நெருநற்றுச் சென்றார்எம் காதலர் யாமும்
எழுநாளேம் மேனி பசந்து.

nerunaṟṟuc ceṉṟār'em kātalar yāmum
eḻunāḷēm mēṉi pacantu

1279. தொடிநோக்கி மென்தோளும் நோக்கி அடிநோக்கி
அஃதாண் டவள்செய் தது.

toṭinōkki meṉtōḷum nōkki aṭinōkki
aḥtāṇ ṭavaḷcey tatu

1280. பெண்ணினால் பெண்மை உடைத்தென்ப கண்ணினால்
காமநோய் சொல்லி இரவு.

peṇṇiṉāl peṇmai uṭaitteṉpa kaṇṇiṉāl
kāmanōy colli iravu

1276. He showers me with endearments,
pleasures me intensely – making me
feel (that soon) I will be surrounded
by the lack of his love (his parting).

1277. My bangles perceived,
even before I did, the news
of the impending departure
of my man of these cold shores.

1278. Just yesterday
my lover went away—
My skin betrays the sorrow
of seven long days.

1279. Speaking with her eyes,
she pointed at her bangles,
her slender shoulders, her feet—
This is all that she did.

1280. She begs with her eyes,
which speak of how she aches
for sex – it is said, then –
the woman is being womanly.

புணர்ச்சிவிதும்பல்

Longing for Sex

1281. உள்ளக் களித்தலும் காண மகிழ்தலும்
கள்ளுக்கில் காமத்திற் குண்டு.

uḷḷak kaḷittalum kāṇa makiḻtalum
kaḷḷukkil kāmattiṟ kuṇṭu

1282. தினைத்துணையும் ஊடாமை வேண்டும் பனைத்துணையும்
காமம் நிறைய வரின்.

tiṉaittuṇaiyum ūṭāmai vēṇṭum paṉaittuṇaiyum
kāmam niṟaiya variṉ

1283. பேணாது பெட்பவே செய்யினும் கொண்கனைக்
காணா தமையல கண்.

pēṇātu peṭpavē ceyyiṉum koṇkaṉaik
kāṇā tamaiyala kaṇ

1284. ஊடற்கண் சென்றேன்மன் தோழி அதுமறந்து
கூடற்கண் சென்றதுஎன் நெஞ்சு.

ūṭaṟkaṇ ceṉṟēṉmaṉ tōḻi atumaṟantu
kūṭaṟkaṇ ceṉṟatu'eṉ neñcu

1285. எழுதுங்கால் கோல்காணாக் கண்ணேபோல் கொண்கன்
பழிகாணேன் கண்ட இடத்து.

eḻutuṅkāl kōlkāṇāk kaṇṇēpōl koṇkaṉ
paḻikāṇēṉ kaṇṭa iṭattu

1281. Not wine
but it is sex that gives
sheer delight at thought
and such pleasure at sight.

1282. No, not even a little-millet pout –
total non-sulking is essential
when sexual desire overflows
and stands as tall as a palmyra.

1283. He does not care for me,
he does just as he pleases;
yet my eyes know no peace,
not having seen my man.

1284. Petulant, I went to pick
a fight, dear girlfriend –
but my heart forgot that,
and ran after him for sex.

1285. Like eyes that cannot see
a kohl-liner while it defines them,
I do not see my lover's faults
when he is in front of me.

1286. காணுங்கால் காணேன் தவறாய காணாக்கால்
காணேன் தவறல் லவை.

kāṇuṅkāl kāṇēṉ tavaṟāya kāṇākkāl
kāṇēṉ tavaṟal lavai

1287. உய்த்தல் அறிந்து புனல்பாய் பவரேபோல்
பொய்த்தல் அறிந்தென் புலந்து.

uyttal aṟintu puṉalpāy pavarēpōl
poyttal aṟinteṉ pulantu

1288. இளித்தக்க இன்னா செயினும் களித்தார்க்குக்
கள்ளற்றே கள்வநின் மார்பு.

iḷittakka iṉṉā ceyiṉum kaḷittārkkuk
kaḷḷaṟṟē kaḷvaniṉ mārpu

1289. மலரினும் மெல்லிது காமம் சிலர்அதன்
செவ்வி தலைப்படு வார்.

malariṉum mellitu kāmam cilar'ataṉ
cevvi talaippaṭu vār

1290. கண்ணின் துனித்தே கலங்கினாள் புல்லுதல்
என்னினும் தான்விதுப் புற்று.

kaṇṇiṉ tuṉittē kalaṅkiṉāḷ pullutal
eṉṉiṉum tāṉvitup puṟṟu

1286. When he is with me,
I see no faults at all.
When we are apart,
I see nothing but faults.

1287. Like those who dive, aware
they will be dragged away,
I learnt the futility of anger
by fighting with my lover.

1288. Like drink, that reduces
the drunk to objects
of ridicule, so does the
chest of this charmer.

1289. Softer than flowers
is making love...
Few obtain
its elegance.

1290. Her eyes held tears
as she sulked – we hugged,
trembling with desire;
her haste surpassed mine.

நெஞ்சொடுபுலத்தல்

Berating Her Heart

1291. அவர்நெஞ்சு அவர்க்காதல் கண்டும் எவன்நெஞ்சே
நீஎமக்கு ஆகா தது.

avarneñcu avarkkātal kaṇṭum evaṉneñcē
nī'emakku ākā tatu

1292. உறாஅ தவர்க்கண்ட கண்ணும் அவரைச்
செறாஅரெனச் சேறியென் நெஞ்சு.

uṟā'a tavarkkaṇṭa kaṇṇum avaraic
ceṟā'areṉac cēṟiyeṉ neñcu

1293. கெட்டார்க்கு நட்டார்இல் என்பதோ நெஞ்சேநீ
பெட்டாங்கு அவர்பின் செலல்.

keṭṭārkku naṭṭār'il eṉpatō neñcēnī
peṭṭāṅku avarpiṉ celal

1294. இனிஅன்ன நின்னொடு சூழ்வார்யார் நெஞ்சே
துனிசெய்து துவ்வாய்காண் மற்று.

iṉi'aṉṉa niṉṉoṭu cūḻvāryār neñcē
tuṉiceytu tuvvāykāṇ maṟṟu

1295. பெறாஅமை அஞ்சும் பெறின்பிரிவு அஞ்சும்
அறாஅ இடும்பைத்தென் நெஞ்சு.

peṟā'amai añcum peṟiṉpirivu añcum
aṟā'a iṭumpaitteṉ neñcu

1291. Having seen how his heart
is in love with him, dear heart,
whose are you, when you
don't get along with me?

1292. Having seen he cannot
come close or commit,
my heart takes no offence;
it still goes in search of him.

1293. It is said: 'The ruined have
no friends.' Is what why,
my heart, you abandon me
and run after him?

1294. First, sulk and refuse; then,
yield and enjoy. You failed
to follow this. Who will now
rally around you, my heart?

1295. The fear of not attaining my lover
and, after having him, the fear
of separation – my heart lives
in this perpetual agony.

1296. தனியே இருந்து நினைத்தக்கால் என்னைத்
தினிய இருந்ததென் நெஞ்சு.

taṉiyē iruntu niṉaittakkāl eṉṉait
tiṉiya iruntateṉ neñcu

1297. நாணும் மறந்தேன் அவர்மறக் கல்லாஎன்
மாணா மடநெஞ்சிற் பட்டு.

nāṇum maṟantēṉ avarmaṟak kallā'eṉ
māṇā maṭaneñciṟ paṭṭu

1298. எள்ளின் இளிவாம்என்று எண்ணி அவர்திறம்
உள்ளும் உயிர்க்காதல் நெஞ்சு.

eḷḷiṉ iḷivāmeṉṟu eṇṇi avartiṟam
uḷḷum uyirkkātal neñcu

1299. துன்பத்திற்கு யாரே துணையாவார் தாமுடைய
நெஞ்சந் துணையல் வழி.

tuṉpattiṟku yārē tuṇaiyāvār tāmuṭaiya
neñcan tuṇaiyal vaḻi

1300. தஞ்சம் தமரல்லர் ஏதிலார் தாமுடைய
நெஞ்சம் தமரல் வழி.

tañcam tamarallar ētilār tāmuṭaiya
neñcam tamaral vaḻi

1296. Alone, I remained
thinking of him
as my heart kept
at devouring me.

1297. Under the influence
of my shameless, foolish heart,
I forgot all bashfulness, but
I could not forget him.

1298. Caught in the love of its life,
my heart recollects his greatness alone,
because blaming him brings
disgrace upon it.

1299. Who, whoever will be
my companion-in-grief,
when my own heart
refuses to stay with me?

1300. My own heart is not my ally.
Will strangers send
their own heart
my way?

புலவி

Sulking

1301. புல்லா திராஅப் புலத்தை அவர்உறும்
அல்லல்நோய் காண்கம் சிறிது.

pullā tirā'ap pulattai avarur̲um
allalnōy kāṇkam cir̲itu

1302. உப்பமைந் தற்றால் புலவி அதுசிறிது
மிக்கற்றால் நீள விடல்.

uppamain tar̲r̲āl pulavi atucir̲itu
mikkar̲r̲āl nīḷa viṭal

1303. அலந்தாரை அல்லல்நோய் செய்தற்றால் தம்மைப்
புலந்தாரைப் புல்லா விடல்.

alantārai allalnōy ceytar̲r̲āl tam'maip
pulantāraip pullā viṭal

1304. ஊடி யவரை உணராமை வாடிய
வள்ளி முதலரிந் தற்று.

ūṭi yavarai uṇarāmai vāṭiya
vaḷḷi mutalarin tar̲r̲u

1305. நலத்தகை நல்லவர்க்கு ஏஎர் புலத்தகை
பூஅன்ன கண்ணார் அகத்து.

nalattakai nallavark kē'er pulattakai
pūvan̲n̲a kaṇṇār akattu

1301. Stay put, do not embrace
your pouting lover;
let us watch awhile
their distressed state.

1302. Like salt for seasoning,
proportion is everything;
in sulking – a little excess
spoils the taste.

1303. To leave a sulking lover
unembraced
is to inflict hurt
on the grievously injured.

1304. To be unfeeling
to a sulking lover
is to cut a withered
creeper at its root.

1305. Even great, good men
appear fetching when
their flower-eyed beloved
grows petulant.

1306. துனியும் புலவியும் இல்லாயின் காமம்
கனியும் கருக்காயும் அற்று.

tuṉiyum pulaviyum illāyiṉ kāmam
kaṉiyum karukkāyum aṟṟu

1307. ஊடலின் உண்டாங்கோர் துன்பம் புணர்வது
நீடுவ தன்றுகொல் என்று.

ūṭaliṉ uṇṭāṅkōr tuṉpam puṇarvatu
nīṭuva taṉṟukol eṉṟu

1308. நோதல் எவன்மற்று நொந்தாரென்று அஃதறியும்
காதலர் இல்லா வழி.

nōtal evaṉmaṟṟu nontāreṉ ṟaḥtaṟiyum
kātalar illā vaḻi

1309. நீரும் நிழலது இனிதே புலவியும்
வீழுநர் கண்ணே இனிது.

nīrum niḻala tiṉitē pulaviyum
vīḻunar kaṇṇē iṉitu

1310. ஊடல் உணங்க விடுவாரொடு என்நெஞ்சம்
கூடுவேம் என்பது அவா.

ūṭal uṇaṅka viṭuvāroṭu eṉneñcam
kūṭuvēm eṉpa tavā

1306. Desire without daring
lacks the sweet-mellow,
and without sulking
the hard-raw fruits.

1307. A single sorrow surrounds
every lover's strife—
Will this not delay
our having sex?

1308. What is the point
of my dreadful anguish,
if the lover who will notice
such grieving is not around?

1309. Even water tastes
sweet in the shade;
even sulking is sweet
only in the eyes of lovers.

1310. I am angry, my lover leaves me
drooping with dejection –
yet the desire of my heart
is that we come together.

புலவி நுணுக்கம்

The Subtleties of Sulking

1311. பெண்ணியலார் எல்லாரும் கண்ணின் பொதுஉண்பர்
நண்ணேன் பரத்தநின் மார்பு.

peṇṇiyalār ellārum kaṇṇiṉ potu'uṇpar
naṇṇēṉ parattaniṉ mārpu

1312. ஊடி யிருந்தேமாத் தும்மினார் யாம்தம்மை
நீடுவாழ் கென்பாக் கறிந்து.

ūṭi yiruntēmāt tum'miṉār yāmtam'mai
nīṭuvāḻ keṉpāk kaṟintu

1313. கோட்டுப்பூச் சூடினும் காயும் ஒருத்தியைக்
காட்டிய சூடினீர் என்று.

kōṭṭuppūc cūṭiṉum kāyum oruttiyaik
kāṭṭiya cūṭiṉīr eṉṟu

1314. யாரினும் காதலம் என்றேனா ஊடினாள்
யாரினும் யாரினும் என்று.

yāriṉum kātalam eṉṟēṉā ūṭiṉāḷ
yāriṉum yāriṉum eṉṟu

1315. இம்மைப் பிறப்பில் பிரியலம் என்றேனாக்
கண்நிறை நீர்கொண் டனள்.

im'maip piṟappil piriyalam eṉṟēṉāk
kaṇniṟai nīrkoṇ ṭaṉaḷ

1311. Everyone with womanness
publicly feasts their eyes –
but I will not embrace
your debauched chest.

1312. We sat, we sulked, and we said
nothing. He sneezed, knowing well
(that we would break our silence)
we would bless him, saying, 'Long live!'

1313. I wear flowers, fresh off trees;
she burns – 'You wear this
only to show off
to some woman.'

1314. When I said I loved her
more than anyone else,
she sulked, asking,
than whom? than whom?

1315. I said, 'In this birth,
we are inseparable':
tears welled up
in her eyes.

1316. உள்ளினேன் என்றேன்மற் றென்மறந்தீர் என்றென்னைப்
புல்லாள் புலத்தக் கனள்.

uḷḷiṉēṉ eṉṟēṉmaṟ ṟeṉmaṟantīr eṉṟeṉṉaip
pullāḷ pulattak kaṉa

1317. வழுத்தினாள் தும்மினே னாக அழித்தழுதாள்
யாருள்ளித் தும்மினீர் என்று.

vaḻuttiṉāḷ tum'miṉē ṉāka aḻittaḻutāḷ
yāruḷḷit tum'miṉīr eṉṟu

1318. தும்முச் செறுப்ப அழுதாள் நுமர்உள்ளல்
எம்மை மறைத்திரோ என்று.

tum'muc ceṟuppa aḻutāḷ numar'uḷḷal
em'mai maṟaittirō eṉṟu

1319. தன்னை உணர்த்தினும் காயும் பிறர்க்குநீர்
இந்நீரர் ஆகுதிர் என்று.

taṉṉai uṇarttiṉum kāyum piṟarkkunīr
innīrar ākutir eṉṟu

1320. நினைத்திருந்து நோக்கினும் காயும் அனைத்துநீர்
யாருள்ளி நோக்கினீர் என்று.

niṉaittiruntu nōkkiṉum kāyum aṉaittunīr
yāruḷḷi nōkkiṉīr eṉṟu

1316. 'I remembered you,' I said.
'So, that means you had forgotten me,'
she cried and pulled herself away
from embracing me.

1317. I sneezed: she blessed.
Then, erasing her blessings,
she wept: 'Which woman (now)
thought of you, causing your sneeze?'

1318. I suppressed my sneeze;
she cried, 'Are you hiding
from me that your woman
is thinking of you?'

1319. I pacify her:
she burns—
'Is this how you do it
with the others as well?'

1320. I long for her, I gaze at her,
she burns— 'Who is that woman
on your mind, as you take in
every part of me?'

ஊடலுவகை

The Delights of Sulking

1321. இல்லை தவறவர்க்கு ஆயினும் ஊடுதல்
வல்லது அவர்அளிக்கு மாறு.

illai tavaṟavarkku āyiṉum ūṭutal
vallatu avar'aḷikku māṟu

1322. ஊடலின் தோன்றும் சிறுதுனி நல்லளி
வாடினும் பாடு பெறும்.

ūṭaliṉ tōṉṟum ciṟutuṉi nallaḷi
vāṭiṉum pāṭu peṟum

1323. புலத்தலின் புத்தேள்நாடு உண்டோ நிலத்தொடு
நீரியைந் தன்னார் அகத்து.

pulattaliṉ puttēḷnāṭu uṇṭō nilattoṭu
nīriyain taṉṉār akattu

1324. புல்லி விடாஅப் புலவியுள் தோன்றுமென்
உள்ளம் உடைக்கும் படை.

pulli viṭā'ap pulaviyuḷ tōṉṟumeṉ
uḷḷam uṭaikkum paṭai

1325. தவறிலர் ஆயினும் தாம்வீழ்வார் மென்றோள்
அகறலின் ஆங்கொன் றுடைத்து.

tavaṟilar āyiṉum tāmvīḻvār meṉṟōḷ
akaṟaliṉ āṅkoṉ ṟuṭaittu

1321. No, no, he has no faults,
but my sullenness has such strength,
you see – it makes him pay back
with much more, much more love.

1322. In a lover's quarrel,
a little anger does arise –
but it does good: it makes
a fading love bloom afresh.

1323. Is there any celestial world
greater than those of lovers
faking displeasure, their hearts
made for each other, like earth and rain?

1324. The lover's quarrel,
leading to a ceaseless
embrace, is the army
that smashes my heart.

1325. Though he be faultless,
there is something about
swiftly tearing away from
our lover's soft shoulders.

1326. உணலினும் உண்டது அறல்இனிது காமம்
புணர்தலின் ஊடல் இனிது.

uṇaliṉum uṇṭatu aṟaliṉitu kāmam
puṇartaliṉ ūṭal iṉitu

1327. ஊடலில் தோற்றவர் வென்றார் அதுமன்னும்
கூடலிற் காணப் படும்.

ūṭalil tōṟṟavar veṉṟār atumaṉṉum
kūṭaliṟ kāṇap paṭum

1328. ஊடிப் பெறுகுவம் கொல்லோ நுதல்வெயர்ப்பக்
கூடலில் தோன்றிய உப்பு.

ūṭip peṟukuvam kollō nutalveyarppak
kūṭalil tōṉṟiya uppu

1329. ஊடுக மன்னோ ஒளியிழை யாமிரப்ப
நீடுக மன்னோ இரா.

ūṭuka maṉṉō oḷiyiḻai yāmirappa
nīṭuka maṉṉō irā

1330. ஊடுதல் காமத்திற்கு இன்பம் அதற்கின்பம்
கூடி முயங்கப் பெறின்.

ūṭutal kāmattiṟku iṉpam ataṟkiṉpam
kūṭi muyaṅkap peṟiṉ

1326. Lovers' quarrels are sweeter
than love-making itself;
finishing a meal sweeter
than the feast itself.

1327. In a lovers' quarrel,
the loser wins – and
this truth is seen
in the sex.

1328. Will sulking make us
make love – the way sex
makes our foreheads
sweat salt?

1329. My shimmering beloved,
keep on pouting—
Dear night, stay endless
as I plead with her!

1330. Sex takes delight
in sulking, which
delights in
getting sex.

ENDNOTES

1 Some parts of this introduction appear as an essay in the book *Poetry in Transatlantic Translation: Encounters Across Languages*, eds. Zoe Skoulding & Katherine Hedeen (2022), under the title 'Translation as Circuit-Breaking: Towards a Feminist Rendering of the Tamil Classic Tirukkuṟaḷ'.

2 PTI (2018) Dravidian Language Family is 4,500 Years Old: A Study, *The Hindu*, 21 March, https://www.thehindu.com/sci-tech/science/dravidian-language-family-is-4500-years-old-study/article23314180.ece.

3 Akhilesh, K., Pappu, S., Rajapara, H. et al. (2018), Early Middle Palaeolithic culture in India around 385–172 ka reframes Out of Africa models', *Nature* 554, 97–101: https://doi.org/10.1038/nature25444.

4 Meenakshisundaram (1969), quoted in Andronov (1975), 'Problems of the National Language in Tamil Land', Anthropos, 1(2), p. 181.

5 Andronov, M.S. (1975) Problems of the National Language in Tamil Land, *Anthropos*, 1(2), pp. 181–193.

6 Rudolph, L. I. (1983) 'Establishing a Niche for Cultural Policy: An Introduction', Pacific Affairs 56(1), pp. 5–14.

7 Zvelebil, K. (1973) *The Smile of Murugan: On Tamil Literature of South India* (Leiden, E.J. Brill), p. 4.

8 Zvelebil (1973), p. 12.

9 For a detailed discussion on this, see N. Cutler (1992) 'The Role of Commentary in the Creation of a Text', *Journal of the American Oriental Society*, 112(4), pp. 549–566.

10 தருமர் மணக்கும் தாமத்தார் நச்சர்
பரிதி பரிமே லழகர்-மல்லர்
பரிப்பெருமாள் காலிங்கர், வள்ளுவர்நூற்கு
எல்லையுரை செய்தா ரிவர்.

The commentators who lived between the tenth and thirteenth centuries CE are Manakkudavar, Dhamattar, Nacchar, Paridhi, Pariperumal, Tirumalaiyar, Mallar, Kaalingar, Dharumar, and Parimēlaḻakar.

11 See Cutler (1992) for more on the commentaries.

12 Caṅkam (classical) Tamil poetry traditions are classified into two broad themes: akam (interior) and puṟam (exterior poems), and can also be read as 'home' and 'the world'. For a better understanding, read A.K. Ramanujan (2006) *Poems of Love and War: From the Eight Anthologies and the Ten Long Poems of Classical Tamil* (New Delhi, OUP India).

13 It is also remarkable to realise that all the books in print today follow the arrangement of Parimēlaḻakar. François Gros writes:

> When we pore over the existing commentaries to the *Book of Love*, we immediately notice, with regard to the economy of the work, an almost total consensus on the number, title, and sequence of chapters, and the choice of distiches that each groups together. On the other hand, the arrangement of the distiches within each chapter is astonishingly variable; it continues to be surprising that in a text so much studied that arrangement has not sparked off more interest among critics. Parimēlaḻakar, however, whose text has so much authority that it is practically the only one on sale, and, too, is the only one whose numberation, and therefore arrangement, is followed by all the collective editions which gather together the texts of other commentators, but always according to his, that is: in the inverse order of chronological appearance. Parimēlaḻakar is thus often alone in his opinion. Of the 250 distiches, only five, that is, one out of fifty (of which three are at the beginning of chapters) are in the same place within a chapter according to all the commentators. Not more than a dozen follow the order advocated by Parimēlaḻakar in four commentaries out of five, while thirteen, and among them the last chapter in its entirety, are unanimously placed in the same rank, distinct from the order prescribed by Parimēlaḻakar.

Gros argues that the 'authority conferred on Parimēlaḻakar has too easily devalued the textual tradition anterior to him: a tradition no one has bothered to know or research'. See Gros, F. (2009) *Deep Rivers: Selected Writing on Tamil Literature* (Paris, Institut français de Pondichéry), p. 162.

14 Gros (2009), p. 125.

15 The High Court judge also exempted the teaching of the Iṉpattuppāl, the love poetry of the Tirukkuṟaḷ, in schools – more evidence of the increasing marginalisation of a section of this text.

16 Writing on the nature of the textual material, Zvelebil notes:

> The leaf used is that of *Corypha umbraculifera Linn.* (Skt. *tali,* Ta. *tiiji, ōai),* Engl. talipot. The majority of later and modern manuscripts are either of this leaf, or of the leaf of *Borassus flabelliformis Linn.* (Skt. *tiila,* Ta. *paṉai*), Engl. palmyra(h). The leaves of corypha are larger, thinner, and more flexible, as well as being more durable. The leaves are treated so that ultimately (after a process of selection, cutting, drying and clipping) the right size and shape are obtained; with corypha leaves this may be *ca.* 90 X 8–9 cm, with borassus *ca.* 50–60 X 3–4 cm. The leaves of a 'book' are perforated in one, two, or three places (on the left side, about the middle, and on the right side, depending on their length), and held together by a string running through the holes, which ends with a small knot or an object too large to pass through the holes (a shell, a wooden peg, a button, a piece of metal, or a splinter of the palm-leaf). The string passes through the second and/or third hole and is then wound round the leaves which are finally placed between two small wooden planks or fragments of dry petioles of the palm or, rarely, between ivory plates. The palm-leaves prepared for writing are termed *etu;* a group of leaves dealing with a particular subject, a palm-leaf 'book' is termed *cuvaṭi* or *ettuccuvati.* The writing on a palm-leaf was effected with a stylus (Skt. *śalāka,* Ta. *eḻuttāṇi*) which engraved the letters on the surface of the leaf; it was held vertically in the right hand while the left, holding the leaf, slowly moved it to the left. To facilitate reading, the leaf was then besmeared with soot or pulverized charcoal mixed with a vegetable juice so that the black mixture remained in the grooves. The lines run parallel with the length of the leaves. On certain leaves which are very long, or in certain Tamil texts in verse, the lines are grouped in two or three columns. Around the holes, and along the margins, the space is usually left blank. The commentaries were usually written above or below the text, or even around the basic text

which was written in larger characters. The pagination is in the right margin.

See Zvelebil, K. (1992) *Companion Studies to the History of Tamil Literature* (Leiden, E.J. Brill), pp. 41–42.

17 The authors' intention was to popularise these ancient scripts and to increase common the people's ability to read them. The usage of the Tirukkuṟaḷ in this endeavour shows how universal a text it is in the Tamil sphere. It is an invaluable resource to trace how the language's script has evolved.

18 Quoted in Zvelebil (1992), p. 43.

19 This is independently corroborated by other commentators such as the poet, professor and scholar A.K. Ramanujan, quoted in Zvelebil (1992), p. 47. Another factor for ancient literature being hidden in the limbo of oblivion was the strong and lasting influence of militant Brahminical Hinduism. The later medieval Saiva and Vaiṣṇavite scholars 'apparently tabooed as irreligious all secular texts, which included the earliest and the greatest of Tamil literary texts; they disallowed from study all Jain and Buddhist texts' (Zvelebil, 1973, p. 268).

20 Gover, cited in Zvelebil, K. (1992) *Companion Studies to the History of Tamil Literature* (Leiden, E.J. Brill), p. 46. Zvelebil further adds: 'The whole problem of wilful destruction, ideological interpolations, interference and "corruption" of ancient Tamil texts is a matter which certainly needs further independent investigation' (p. 47).

21 இருபுனலும் வாய்ந்த மலையும் வருபுனலும்
வல்லரணும் நாட்டிற்கு உறுப்பு.

irupuṉalum vāynta malaiyum varupuṉalum
vallaraṇum nāṭṭiṟku uṟuppu.

A land's limbs are waters from rains,
Springs and well placed hills, and strong fortress.

See Iravatam Mahadevan, 'Tiruvaḷḷuvariṉ tirumēṉi tāṅkiya taṅkakkācu – 2' ('The Golden Coin bearing the image of Tiruvalluvar'), www.varalaaru.com/design/article.aspx?ArticleID=539.

22 For a thorough history of the translations and a compilation of 18 translations in English of each kuṟaḷ, please refer to A.A. Manavalan, ed. (2010) *A Compendium of Tirukkuṟaḷ Translation in English* (Chennai, Central Institute of Classical Tamil).

23 Pope, G.U. (1886) *The 'Sacred' Kurral of Tiruvalluva-Nayanar* (Tiruvalluvanayanar arulicceyta Tirrukkural) (London, W.H. Allen), accessible at https://archive.org/details/tiruvalluvanayanootiruuoft.

24 Sage Valluvar, priest of thy lowly clan,
No tongue repeats, no speech reveals thy name;
Yet, all things changing, dieth not thy fame,
For thou art bard of universal man;

And still thy 'book' above the waters wan,
Virtue, true wealth, and joy, and being's aim,
In sweetest mystic couplets doth proclaim,
Where winds sea-wafted palmy forests fan.

Haply undreamed of 'visions' glad thine eyes
In realms beyond thy fabled 'seven-fold birth',
And clouds of darkness from thy spirit roll;

While lands far off have heard with strange surprise
Faint echoes of thy song. Through all the earth
Men hail thee, brother, seer of spotless soul.

Pope (1886), p. ii.

25 Pope (1886), p.iii.

26 Valentine Daniel (1989) 'Three Dispositions towards the Past: One Sinhala, Two Tamil, Social Analysis', *The International Journal of Anthropology*, September, No. 25, pp. 22–41.

27 Pope (1886), pp. i–ii.

28 Bosco, D. (2022) 'Tamil Nadu: Chidambaram Priests Again Refuse to Show Account', *Times of India*, 9 June, https://timesofindia.indiatimes.com/city/chennai/tamil-nadu-chidambaram-priests-again-refuse-to-show-accounts/articleshow/92091583.cms.

29 Singaravel, B. (2022) 'Chidambaram Temple Priests Booked for Castist Slurs against Dalit Woman Devotee', *The News Minute*, 18 February, https://www.thenewsminute.com/article/chidambaram-temple-priests-booked-casteist-slurs-against-dalit-woman-devotee-161134.

30 Albertine Gaur (1966) 'A Catalogue of B. Ziegenbalg's Tamil Library', *The British Museum Quarterly*, Spring, 30(3/4), pp. 99–105.

31 Sweetman, W. (2019) 'The Absent Vedas', *Journal of the American Oriental Society*, 139(4), pp. 781–803.

32 Sweetman, W. (2019) The Absent Vedas, *Journal of the American Oriental Society*, 139(4), pp. 781–803.

33 V.R. Ramachandra Dikshitar (1944), Tirukkural (Madras, The Adyar Library and Research Centre); available digitally at: https://archive.org/details/in.ernet.dli.2015.24915.

34 Cutler (1992), pp. 549–566.

35 For more on this, I highly recommend Sumathi Ramaswamy (1997) *Passions of the Tongue: Language Devotion in Tamil India*, 1891–1970 (Berkeley, University of California Press).

36 Veeramani, K. Ed. (2019) *The Collected Works of Thanthai Periyar E.V. Ramasamy, "Thirukkural: Valluvar"*, Vol. 37 (Chennai, Periyar Self-Respect Propaganda Institution), p. 153.

37 Periyar's speech at a meeting on 17 January 1949.

38 Veeramani (2019), Vol. 37, p. 94.

39 Express News Service (2019) 'Archaeologist R Nagaswamy Refutes Stalin's Charges', *The New Indian Express*, 8 March, https://www.newindianexpress.com/states/tamil-nadu/2019/mar/08/archaeologist-refutes-stalins-charges-1948272.html.

40 Nagaswamy cites Pope's writings to say that Tirukkuṟaḷ originated from the Vedas. However, Pope has this to say: 'It is not probable that Tiruvalluvar translated a cloka from Sanskrit' (1886, p. iv), and also: 'The Kurral is composed in pure Tamil, that is, with scarcely any admixture of Sanskrit. This will appear from the Vocabulary and Concordance, which will enable the student to form an independent judgement on many points of grammar. Tamil is not a dialect of Sanskrit, but an independent language with a copious and original vocabulary, having a very clear and philosophical grammatical system, very highly cultivated, and in every respect equal to Sanskrit itself' (ibid., p. xv).

41 Periyar E.V. Ramasamy (2007), 'Why Were Women Enslaved', Periyar Self Respect Propaganda Society, Chennai.

42 Pope (1886), p. xiii.

43 Zvelebil (1973), p. 166.

44 Gros (2009), p. 124.

45 Zvelebil (1974), who holds that there are no structural gaps in the Tirukkuṟaḷ, also states that every kuṟaḷ has 'two kinds of meaning: its own intrinsic and isolated meaning, and the additional structural meaning in relation to other couplets and to the entire text which forms a perfect

total structure'. In Zvelebil's opinion, the *Tirukkuṟaḷ* 'is no anthology of isolated aphorisms. If no replacement of any semantic element, however small, will do in a text where a single alteration will transform or destroy it, how can one expect to have an adequate translation?' For Zvelebil the work is untranslatable (at least, impossible to translate adequately), and François Gros — who reordered the kuṟaḷs and comes from the opposite end of the spectrum as far as chapter/verse order is concerned – shares his point of view. Gros's argument for why the text defies translation arises from the 'formal perfection of the work' (Gros, 2009, p. 125). See also Zvelebil (1974), p. 120.

46 For more on the transgressions of Parimēlaḻakar, I suggest the reader refer to Cutler (1992) and Gros (2009).

47 Gros (2009), p. 139.

GALLEY BEGGAR PRESS

We hope that you've enjoyed *The Book of Desire*. If you would like to find out more about our authors, head to www.galleybeggar.co.uk.

There, you will also find information about our subscription scheme, 'Galley Buddies', which is there to ensure we can continue to put out ambitious and unusual books like *The Book of Desire*.

Subscribers to Galley Beggar Press:

- Receive limited black cover editions of our future titles (printed in a one-time run of 600).
- Have their names included in a special acknowledgement section at the back of our books.
- Are sent regular updates and invitations to our book launches, talks and other events.
- Enjoy a 20% discount code for the purchase of any of our backlist (as well as for general use throughout our online shop).

WHY BE A GALLEY BUDDY?

At Galley Beggar Press we don't want to compromise on the excellence of the writing we put out, or the physical quality of our books. We've also enjoyed numerous successes and prize nominations since we set up in 2012. Almost all of our authors have gone on to be longlisted, shortlisted, or the winners of over twenty of the world's most prestigious literary awards.

But publishing for the sake of art is a risky commercial strategy. In order to keep putting out the very best books we can, and to continue to support talented writers, we need your help. The money we receive from our Galley Buddy scheme is an essential part of keeping us going.

By becoming a Galley Buddy, you help us to launch and foster a new generation of writers.

To join today, head to:
https://www.galleybeggar.co.uk/subscribe

FRIENDS OF GALLEY BEGGAR PRESS

Galley Beggar Press would like to thank the following individuals, without the generous support of whom our books would not be possible:

Cameron Adams
Muriel Adams
Kémy Ade
Timothy Ahern
Liz Aiken
Sam Ainsworth
Jez Aitchison
Richard Allen
Lulu Allison
Adrian Alvarez
Anna Andreou
Simon Andrup
Jerome Anello
Natalia Anjaparidze
Kirk Annett
Deborah Arata
Robert Armiger
Kate Armstrong
Sean Arnold
Curt Arnson
Jake Arthur
Xanthe Ashburner
Bethany Ashley
Robert Ashton
Rachel Atkin
Edmund Attrill
Valda Aviks
Jo Ayoubi
Kerim Aytec
Claire Back
Thomas Badyna
Andrew Bailey
Dexter Bailey
Tom Bailey
Edward Baines
Glynis Baker
James Baker
John Balfour
Maggie Balistreri
Christopher Ball
Andrew Ballantyne
Sarah Balstrup
Paul Bangert
Victoria Barkas
Andrea Barlien
Chad Barnes
Kevin Barrett
Matthew Barron
Phil Bartlett
Morgan Baxley
Perry Beadsworth
Rachael Beale
Rebecca Bealey
Lauren Beattie
James Beavis
Rachel Bedder
Georgia Beddoe
Joseph Bell
Angel Belsey
Madeline Bennett
Felicity Bentham
Jean Bergin
Michelle Best
Gary Betts
David Bevan
Allison Beynon
Alison Bianchi
Gavin Bingham
Sandra Birnie
Donna-Louise Bishop
Nick Black
Mark Blackburn
Peter Blackett
Matt Blackstock
Kate Bland
Melissa Blaschke
Charlie Bloor
Blue and Kat
Lynne Blundell
David Boddy
Sophie Boden
Rich Boden
John Bogg
Kalina Borisova
Poppy Boutell
Edwina Bowen

Mark Bowles
Michelle Bowles
David Bowman
Joanna Bowman
Alexander Bown
Matthew Boyd
Astrid Bracke
David Bradley
Sean Bradley
David Brady
Debby Brady
Joan Brennan
Andrew J. Bremner
Chris Brewer
Amanda Bringans
Erin Britton
Julia Brocking
Dean Brooks
Anthony Brown
Lily Brown
Peter Brown
Sheila Browse
Carrie Brunt
Richard Bryant
Lesley Budge
Daniel Bugg
Laura Bui
Gayle Burgoyne
Tony Burke
Kevin Burrell
Tamsin Bury
Joe Butler
Esther van Buul
Gosia Buzzanca
Sarah Brayshaw
Andrew Bremner
Kester Brewin
Barry Bryne
Barbara Byar
Jorien Caers
Alan Calder
June Caldwell
Matt Callow
Francesca Cambridge Mallen
Gordon Cameron
Mark Campbell
Laura Canning
Annette Capel
Rhian Capener
Andrew Cardus
Ros Carne
Jackie Carpenter
Leona Carpenter
Daniel Carr
Sean Carroll
Shaun Carter
Stuart Carter
Liam Casey
David Caves
Leigh Chambers
Sonia Chander
John Chapman
Richard Chatterton
Christel Chen
Lina Christopoulou
Neal Chuang
Gemma Church
Neil Churchill
Jack Clark
Deborah Ann Clarke
Simon Clarke
Douglas Clarke-Williams
Rex Cleaver
Steve Clough
Emily Coghill
Steven Coghill
Daniel Cohen
Paul Cole
Faith Coles
John Coles
Emma Coley
Sam Coley
Jonathan Collings
X Collins
Jess Conway
Joe Cooney
Sarah Corbett
Sarah Corrie
Paul Corry
Andy Corsham
Mary Costello
Sally Cott
Nick Coupe
Diarmuid Cowan
Colette Cox
Isabelle Coy-Dibley
Matthew Craig
Anne Craven
Anne-Marie Creamer
Alan Crilly
Joanna Crispin
Brenda Croskery
Alasdair Cross
James Cross
Jenny Crossland
Kate Crowcroft
Miles Crowley
Stephen Cuckney
John Cullinane

Damian Cummings
Stephen Cummins
Andrew Cupples
TR Currell
Patrick Curry
Emma Curtis Lake
Chris Cusack
Will Dady
Siddharth Dalal
Jon Dalladay
Rupert Dastur
Maurizio Dattilo
Sally Davenport
Claudia Daventry
Andrew Davies
Julie Davies
Linda Davies
Nickey Davies
Ian Daw
Emilie Day
Emily Day
Toby Day
Sarah Deacon
Ann Debono
Meaghan Delahunt
Rebecca Demaree
Stanislaus Dempsey
Paul Dettmann
Angelica Diehn
Jane Dietrich
Kasper Dijk
Gary Dixon
Turner Docherty
William Dobson
Mark Dolan
Freda Donoghue
Dennis Donothan
Laura Donovan
Kirsty Doole
Oliver Dorostkar
David Douce
Janet Dowling
Kelly Downey
Jamie Downs
Iain Doyle
Alan Duckers
Ian Dudley
Fiona Duffy
Anthony Duncan
Stanka Easton
Matthew Eatough
Nicola Edwards
Lance Ehrman
Jonathan Elkon
Ian Ellison
Thomas Ellmer
Theresa Emig
Stefan Erhardt
Fiona Erskine
Frances Evangelista
Gareth Evans
Kieran Evans
Paul Ewen
Adam Fales
Sarah Farley
Pauline Farrar
Emma Feather
Lori Feathers
Gerard Feehily
Jeremy Felt
Victoria Fendall
Maria Guilliana Fenech
Michael Fenton
Edward J. Field
Paul Fielder
Catriona Firth
Becky Fisher
Duncan Fisher
Nicholas Fisher
Caitlin Fitzgerald
Judith Flanders
Mark Flaum
Grace Fletcher-Hackwood
Hayley Flockhart
Nicholas Flower
Patrick Foley
James Fourniere
Ceriel Fousert
Kathleen Fox
Richard Fradgley
Matthew Francis
Nigel Francis
Bridget Fraser
Emily Fraser
Charlotte Frears
Emma French
Ruth Frendo
Elizabeth Frye
Gill Fryzer
Graham Fulcher
Paul Fulcher
Jane Fuller
Stephen Furlong
Michael Furness
Richard Furniss
John Gallagher
Timothy Gallimore
Marc Galvin
Annabel Gaskell

Nolan Geoghegan
Pia Ghosh Roy
Phil Gibby
Alison Gibson
Luke Gibson
Jacqueline Gittens
James Goddard
Stephanie Golding
Elizabeth Goldman
Morgan Golf-French
Sakura Gooneratne
Sara Gore
Nikheel Gorolay
Cathy Goudie
Simon Goudie
Emily Grabham
Becky Greer
Ben Griffiths
Neil Griffiths
Vicki Grimshaw
Christopher Gruppet
Sam Gugliani
Robbie Guillory
Drew Gummerson
Dave Gunning
Ian Hagues
Daniel Hahn
Callum Hale-Thomson
Nikki Hall
Alice Halliday
Verity Halliday
Peter Halliwell
Emma Hammond
Paul Handley
Rachel Handley
Paul Hanson
Jill Harrison
Greg Harrowing
Alice Harvey
Becky Harvey
Espen Hauglid
Simon Hawkesworth
Connor Hayden
Adrian Hayes
Rachel Heath
David Hebblethwaite
Richard Hemmings
Peter Hemsworth
Petra Hendrickson
Padraig J. Heneghan
Stu Hennigan
Adam Saiz Abo Henriksen
Penelope Hewett-Brown
Felix Hewison-Carter
Simon Higgins
Annette Higgs
Alexander Highfield
Jennifer Hill
Daniel Hillman
David Hirons
Ned Hirst
Marcus Hobson
Jamie Hodder-Williams
Nicholas Hodges
Stephenjohn Holgate
Turan Holland
Aisling Holling
Ben Holloway
David Holmes
Rene Hooft
Adrian Howe
William Hsieh
Steve Hubbard
Hugh Hudson
Anna Jean Hughes
Emily Hughes
Richard Hughes
Robert Hughes
Jon Hulbert
Kim-ling Humphrey
Joanne Humphries
Louise Hussey
LJ Hutchins
Lori Inglis Hall
Grace Iredale
Simon Issatt
Joseph Jackson
Ryan Jackson
Jane Jakeman
Briley James
Hayley James
Helen James
Michael James
Graeme Jarvie
Daniel Jean
Gareth Jelley
Kavita A. Jindal
Rachel John
Alice Jolly
Alex Jones
Bevan Jones
Deborah Jones
Ellen Jones
Jupiter Jones
Rebecca Jones
Amy Jordison
Anna Jordison

Diana Jordison
Atul Joshi
Sapna Joshi
Claire Jost
Rebecca Joy
Benjamin Judge
Gary Kaill
Darren Kane
Thomas Kealy
Andrew Kelly
Emily Kent
Michael Ketchum
Jeffrey Kichen
Ross Kilpatrick
Anna Kime
Fran Kime
Xanath King
Euan Kitson
Clara Knight
Jacqueline Knott
Amy Koheealiee
David Krakauer
Emily Kubisiak
Elisabeth Kumar
Navpreet Kundal
Candida Lacey
Geves Lafosse
Rachel Lalchan
Philip Lane
Dominique Lane-Osherov
I Lang
Kathy Lanzarotti
Kim Laramee
Steven Law
Jo Lawrence
Lorraine Lawrence
Andrew Lawton-Collins
Sue Lawson
Elizabeth Eva Leach
Stephen Leach
Rick Le Coyte
Jessica Leggett
Carley Lee
Liz and Pete Lee
Tracey Lee
Jessica Leggett
Edwin Lerner
Chiara Levorato
Sara Levy
Elizabeth Leyland
Oliver Lewis
Yin Lim
Chris Lintott
Clayton Lister
Amy Lloyd
Lyn Lockwood
Katie Long
Tracey Longworth
Nikyta Loraine
Zoe Lourie
Kathryn Lovell
Lele Lucas
John Lutz
Michael Lynch
Marc Lyth
Paul McAuley
James McCann
Leona McCann
Chris McLaren
Paul McCombs
Emma McConnell
Fabia McDougall
Grace McHale
Sheila McIntosh
Alan McIntyre
Eleanor McIntyre
Sarah McIntyre
Lucie McKnight Hardy
Gerald McWilliams
Ewan MacDonald
Andrea MacLeod
Victoria MacKenzie
Duncan Mackie
Brendan Madden
Joseph Maffey
Anne Maguire
Sean Maguire
Eleanor Maier
Philip Makatrewicz
Sarah Male
Anil Malhotra
Tom Mandall
Joshua Mandel
Venetia Manning
Chiara Margiotta
John Marr
Natalie Marshall
Paul Marshall
Aoife Martin
Harriet Martin
Iain Martin
William Mascioli
Rachel Mason
Rebecca Masterman
Sarah Maxted
Susan Maxwell
Dan Mayers
Stephen Maynard

Sally Mayor
Jason Merrells
Andy Merrills
Tina Meyer
Lindsey Millen
Michael Millington
Ali Millar
Phillipa Mills
Robert Mills
Sally Minogue
Fiona Mitchell
Lindsay Mitchell
Adam Moliver
Ian Mond
Fiona Mongredien
Alexander Monker
Alex Moore
Clare Moore
Gary Moore
Michelle Moorhouse
Jonathan Moreland
Nigel J. Morgan
Harriet Mossop
Carlos Eduardo Morreo
Elizabeth Morris
Jackie Morris
Joanne Morris
Julie Morris
Patrick Morris
Clive Morrison
Catriona Morrison
Donald Morrison
Penny Morrison
Roger Morrison
Jennifer Mulholland
Christian Murphy
Nicole Murphy
Ben Myers
Electra Nanou
Zosha Nash
Linda Nathan
Tim Neighbour
Marie Laure Neulet
Natalie Newman
Amanda Nicholls
Catherine Nicholson
Sophia Nixon
Mariah de Nor
Emma Norman
Sam North
Calum Novak-Mitchell
Anna Nsubuga
Arif Nurmohamed
Simon Nurse
Rachel Nye
Christopher O'Brien
James O'Brien
Rodney O'Connor
James O'Leary
Alec Olsen
Siobhaan O'Neill
Valerie O'Riordan
Sam Oborne
Liz O'Sullivan
Kate Packwood
Steven Palter
David Parker
Dave Parry
Simon Parsons
Gary Partington
Debra Patek
Ian Patterson
Adam Paxton
Mark Payne
Stephen Pearsall
Rosie Pendlebury
Jonathan Perks
Davide Perottoni
Connor Perrie
Tom Perrin
Robert Perry
Seetal Petal
Tony Pettigrew
Dan Phillips
Fergus Pickles
Hannah Piekarz
Steven Pilling
Robert Pisani
Ben Plouviez
Louise Pointer
Alex Pointon Melville
Dimitrios Polemis
Erin Polmear
James Pomar
Dan Pope
Jonathan Pool
Christopher Potter
Lesley Preston
Libby Preston
David Prince
Victoria Proctor
Jill Propst
James Puddephatt
Alan Pulverness
Lisa Quattromini
Leng Leng Quek
Zoe Radley
Jane Rainbow

Sim Ralph
Polly Randall
Lauren Ravazi
Ian Redfern
Sam Reese
Padraid Reidy
Vasco Resende
Amy Reynolds
Caroline Riddell
Mario Riggio
Alison Riley
Thea Marie Rishovd
Laura Roach
Chris Roberts
Stephen Roberts
Emily Robinsonb
Ada Robinson
Joanna Robinson
Joyce Lillie Robinson
Neil Robinson
Lizz Roe
Lorraine Rogerson
Kalina Rose
Michael Rowley
Nathan Rowley
Martin Rowsell
Beverly Rudy
Giles Ruffer
Naben Ruthnum
John Rutter
Paul Ryan
Amanda Saint
Floriane Sajdak
Alison Sakai
Himanshu Kamal Saliya
Bairbre Samh
Robert Sanderson
Benedict Sangster
Steven Savile
Lior Sayada
Liam Scallon
Amy Scarrott
Linde Schaafsma
Robert Scheffel
Benedict Schofield
Jan Schoones
Ros Schwartz
Craig Scott
Nicola Scott
Stephen Robert Scott
Darren Seeley
Darren Semple
Henry Settle
Elie Sharp
Nicola Shepherd
Emma Shore
Elena Shushakova
Deborah Siddoway
Kate Simpson
Stu Sizer
Ann Slack
Mark Slater
Jay Slayton-Josh
Sarah Slowe
Ben Smith
Catherine Smith
Chris Smith
Hazel Smith
Helen Smith
Ian Smith
Kieron Smith
Nicola Smith
Shannon Smith
Tom Smyth
Haydon Spenceley
Arabella Spencer
Sarah Spitz
S.O. Spitzer
Chiara Spruijt
Levi Stahl
Conor Stait
Ellie Staite
Karl Stange
Daniel Staniforth
Cameron Stark
Phil Starling
Cathryn Steele
Jack Stevens
Zac Stevens
Mark Stevenson
Jow Stewart
Dagmara Stoic
Jamie Stone
Justina Stonyte
Anne Storr
Elizabeth Stott
Julia Stringwell
Andrew Stuart
Daryl Sullivan
Jesse Surridge
Drashti Sutariya
Helen Swain
Ashley Tame
Ewan Tant
Sarah Tapp
Ednyfed Tappy
Justine Taylor
Peter Taylor
Moray Teale
Alan Teder

Gill Thackray
Helen Thain
Darren Theakstone
Cennin Thomas
Sue Thomas
Susannah Thompson
Julian Thorne
Matthew Thrift
Alexander Tilston Fleming
Matthew Tilt
Amie Tolson
James Torrance
Eloise Touni
Kate Triggs
Stefani Tuirigangi
Jojo Tulloh
Steve Tuffnell
Devin Tupper
Mike Turner
Neil Turner
Eleanor Updegraff
Geoffrey Urland
Raminta Uselyte
Francesca Veneziano
Irene Verdiesen
Julia Wait
Susan Walby
Chris Walker
Craig Walker
Phoebe Walker
Stephen Walker
Ben Waller
Anna Walsh
Kevin Walsh
Sinead Walsh
Steve Walsh
Christopher Walthorne
Zhen Wang
Jerry Ward
Kate Ward
Peter Ward
Rachael Wardell
Guy Ware
Darren Waring
Diane Waring
Emma Warnock
Stephanie Wasek
Daniel Waterfield
Chris Watts
Sarah Webb
Ian Webster
Lucy Webster
Adam Welch
Joanna Wellings
Ian Wells
Karl Ruben Weseth
Jo West-Moore
Wendy Whidden
Robert White
Ben Wilder
Kyra Wilder
Gary Wilks
Claire Willerton
Andrea Willett
G Williams
Sharon Williams
Emma Wilson
Sarah Wiltshire
Kyle Winkler
Bianca Winter
Lucie Winter
Sheena Winter
Astrid Maria Wissenburg
Stephen Witkowski
Michael Wohl
Nathan Wood
Sarah Wood
Paul Woodgate
Emma Woolerton
Lorna Wright
Lydia Wynn
Linday Yates
Faye Young
Ian Young
Juliano Zaffino
Vanessa Zampiga
Sylvie Zannier
Rupert Ziziros
Carsten Zwaaneveld